# OCCUPATIONAL STRESS AND COPING STRATEGIES

# OCCUPATIONAL STRESS AND COPING STRATEGIES

*By*

**Dr. (Mrs.) G. Kavitha**
*Lecturer in Commerce*
*Dept. of Commerce(ca)*
*Vellalar College for Women*
*Thindal, Erode-12*
*Tamil Nadu*
*(India)*

**DISCOVERY PUBLISHING HOUSE PVT. LTD.**
**NEW DELHI-110 002**

First Published – 2009

Reprinted – 2025

ISBN: 978-81-8356-448-9



**Occupational Stress and Coping Strategies**

*Published by:*

**DISCOVERY PUBLISHING HOUSE**

4383/4B, Ansari Road, Darya Ganj

New Delhi-110 002 (India)

*Phone*: +91-11-23279245; 23253475; 43596065

*Mobile*: +91 9811179893 / +91 9871656464

*E-mail*: discoverybooksindia@gmail.com

orderdphbooks@gmail.com

namitwasan9@gmail.com

*web*: www.discoverypublishinggroup.com

*Printed at:*

Infinity Imaging Systems

Delhi

# Preface

In order to bring forth a book that would serve both as an investigation and analysis of people employed in various status and their level of stress, focus has been made on real world problems of an individual and the changing work environment, which creates occupational stress among the employees. Simultaneously, the effective tools for managing stress are also dealt with efficiently.

So, the first step in the creation of this book was to develop a clear understanding of the question, "Why Study Stress Management"? There are many reasons for the study of stress management, but a few of them are so critical to the development of occupational stress and its effect on human skill.

The second reason for studying stress management is the realization that most of mankind's endeavors are channeled through a growing variety of organisations. And these organizations – Government, corporations, Educational institutions, hospitals and so on – are becoming larger and more complex in the current scenario, which compounds the challenge of managing them effectively in the prevailing stiff competition. This situation indirectly increase the working hours, face constant dead lines, and are subject to press we to increase income while keeping cost in check. To do things faster and better, but with fewer people is the goal of many companies. The results can indeed be increased performance, higher profit, and faster growth. But stress, burnout, Aggression and other unpleasant side effects can also occur (both physically & psychologically). The author organized all the reasons and causes for development stress in an orderly way.

Still, another reason for the study of occupational stress is to find better ways an means for avoiding/reducing stress. The author suggested appropriate strategies to eliminate or control organizational – level stress. Further, healthy organizational tips (change) also suggested to reduce the stress.

Indeed it is difficult task to present all the basic essential aspects of such a vast subject like stress management into a limited number of chapters and pages of a brief text. However, an attempt is being made to present what is essential both from the angle of scope of the subject as well as the needs and demands of the scholars and practitioners.

Throughout the book, I have made the subject as readable and stimulating as possible. Each chapter has been provided with a compact and concise summary along with the relevant references.

I deem it a honour and privilege to place my deep sense of gratitude to my research guide *Dr. (Mrs.) V.K. SHOBANA, M.Com., M.Phil., Ph.D.,* Reader in Commerce, Vellalar College for Women, Erode, for her inspiring guidance, valuable suggestions and constant encouragement with utmost care and patience at every state of my research work.

**Dr. KAVITHA G.**

# Contents

# Chapter–1

# INTRODUCTION AND DESIGN OF THE STUDY

## INTRODUCTION

Stress refers to an individual's reaction to a disturbing factor in the environment. It is an adaptive response to an external situation that results in physical, psychological and behavioural deviations for organisational participants. Stress is the result of a mismatch between the challenges experienced and belief in the ability to cope. The challenges may come from external sources and may be the result of too much or too little pressure. They may also come from within the individuals and be the product of their own value systems, needs and expectations. Stress implies some form of demand on the individual, it can be perceived as a threat that it may create a psychological imbalance and can certainly affect individual performance. It is particularly concerned with how people cope with the changes in their lives at work, at home and in other circumstances.

Banking is a service industry and delivers its service across the counter to the ultimate customer. The activities of banking industry are all about 'relationship'. Hence, human resource assumes a very important role in banking industry for providing better services to the customers with a smile in order to cultivate and maintain long lasting relationship with their customers. Notwithstanding the level of technology, banking primarily is a labour intensive service sector; hence it will not be possible for the banks to sustain effectiveness unless the work force is in a stress free and satisfied work environment.

The human resource is termed as total knowledge, skill creation, effective and efficient decision making abilities, talents, value, belief, aptitude and commitment of individual and group involved in and concerned with an organisation. Human resource is the primary capital and all other tangible assets are secondary. The human resource is the most important element for the progress of banking. Though technology can replace manual intervention, the thinking process is the exclusive preserve of human beings. With changing times and technology, banks would require employees with special skills. It is a recognised fact that human resources occupy a unique and sensitive position in banking sector; no meaningful change is possible without the involvement of their employees.

Whenever increased demand in work beyond one's capacity is made, the person is said to be under stress. Stress leads to strain. Stress is felt at the psychological level leading to strain which is felt at the physical level. Irrespective of the profession in which they are engaged in or the status of their official hierarchy or the strata of society to which they belong, people experience stress and strain. Stress could be a stimulating experience as long as it is within a controllable limit. When it goes beyond this limit, stress becomes distress, difficult to be managed. When this happens, the situation becomes hopeless and people feel helpless.

Individual's actions then become dull and everything will appear to go wrong. This situation leads to reducing his efficiency and effectiveness in playing the role assigned to him in the family or society or workplace. His effectiveness may rise up to a particular level of stress, but beyond that level, it invariably drops. Stress arises essentially from his way of responding to a particular situation. There are two types of stress, namely positive and negative.

Positive stress offers potential gain leading to better performance as in the case of an athlete who often uses stress positively and performs better. Negative stress is associated with constraints. When an event or situation is very serious or dangerous, the emotions become negative and create deep dejection, despondency and depression. These negative emotions have a crippling effect on work and life styles.

The root cause of one's emotional problem lies within an individual. It is one's response to the events and not the events themselves which cause misery and grief. Human beings are normally subjected to a set of behavioural attitudes even from childhood duly influenced by parents, teachers, elders, etc. In other words, certain norms of behaviour are imposed on people and they pick up some beliefs concerning their life style. Over a period of time some of these beliefs get further reinforced and they become a part of their personality. If these beliefs are examined, it can be found that many of them may be irrational beliefs. These irrational beliefs which an individual holds influence his mind and create emotional problems. In the work environment, when people feel unable to exert any control or influence over the demands placed upon them, a sort of tension is created that may result in stress.

Stressors can be physical and emotional, internally or externally generated. They can be events, situations, people or demands the individual perceives to be the source of stress. The recognised causes of job stress are numerous and these include work practices, pressure, management techniques and work environment. Researches have shown that there is a very strong link between stress and personal health and they can play a major role in determining the physical and psychological health of an individual as well as success of an organisation. The impact on the organisation could be detrimental and could range from high turnover, absenteeism and poor performance.

Stress can also be created in situations where there are no clear job descriptions or career prospect is absent. Also a lack of understanding of the superiors by the employees and vice versa can exacerbate stress levels. Long tasks may further incubate heavy responsibilities with no authority or decision making, discretion and inadequate time to complete tasks to personal or company standards may also create a stressful situation for an individual. Other possible causes of work related stress may be due to lack of recognition or reward for good job performance, the absence of opportunity to voice complaints and the chances for small error or momentary lapse of attention to have serious or even disastrous consequences. Generally a stressful circumstance is one with which an individual is unable to cope successfully and thus results in unwanted physical, mental or emotional responses.

Stress is a part of everybody's life. Depending on the level of stress it can badly affect one's life especially at the work place where he begins to spend several long hours and thus have less time for other things. Stressed employees may be unhappy and thus produce nominally. Stress can deteriorate social and family relationships and eventually burn one out, taking a toll of one's health, therefore organisations need to recognise stress as a problem and take necessary steps to act upon it. Stress can cause poor work performance and lower employee morale. These factors, in turn, increase employee turnover rate and lessen quality of life.

## STATEMENT OF THE PROBLEM

In today's turbulent business environment, all ambitious and hard working executives, managers and professionals face constant problems and stress in their jobs. Stress has become a major buzzword and legitimate concern of the times.

Stress can have serious consequences on individual's health and work performance. The problems due to high levels of stress can be exhibited physically or behaviourally by the individual. Stress can cause depression, irritation, anxiety, fatigue and reduced job satisfaction. Stress affects individual's performance and effectiveness. It can undermine their relationship at home and on the job. Job stress has been proven to be a difficult issue for the occupational health of the community.

High levels of stress adversely affect physical health and psychological well-being and many aspects of performance. This evidence makes a strong case for understanding and examining occupational stress.

Research studies show that conflicting demands cause confusion among employees and lead to the creation of stressful situations. Multiple pressures or pressures that are unremitting or prolonged may also form the cause for work related stress. Prolonged conflict between individuals is another serious cause for work related stress. In addition to that exposure to prejudice regarding one's age, or gender, will form another major cause of work related stress. When people go to their jobs knowing that they are going to spend a large part of their day in a hostile environment, this will consequently put pressure on them.

Everybody is different and responding differently to stressors. What causes one person to stress out can be a relaxation to another. Certain people have personality traits that cause them over-respond to stressful events. Thus personality plays an important role but often an unpredictable one when it comes to understanding individual's behaviour in occupational settings. Personality traits are very important in the determination of stress levels in an individual. The link between personality and individual health are of great relevance to organisational health.

In relation to the different sources of stress and the different personality characteristics, another element of stress-related outcomes is the way an individual copes and manages stress. Studies indicate that certain groups of people are more vulnerable to the effects of stress. Different people use different ways of trying to cope with stress. According to management experts the best method of stress management depends on both the organisation and the individuals.

Stress is becoming increasingly global and affects all categories of employees in all countries. Because of this, stress and coping with stress have become important concerns both in research and organisational practices.

Absenteeism, poor turnover in work, job dissatisfaction, less commitment to the job and poor performance, moodiness, fatigue, anxiety, frustration and guilt are caused by such stress. It is necessary to tackle effectively the mental and physical stress in order to have better health and living.

Ever increasing demands of a highly competitive work environment in banks require constant updating of knowledge and skills of managers to be able to function effectively. Coupled with this is the need to deal with uncertainties and ambiguity when one cannot rely on past experiences alone to tackle the present problems. Moreover, banks are not able to provide all the learning opportunities needed to today's managers and other employees and that puts the onus of personal growth and development for enhancing the competencies on the employees themselves. It may be because modern technology has made the life of man more complex, full of the hazards of his own creation.

The present era is considered an era of strain, frustration, conflict, tension, depression, psychosomatic diseases and anxiety, which have become regular features of life. Arising both at work and home, these conditions have a detrimental effect on the behaviour of people, which ultimately result in organisational inefficiency and sickness. Banking industry is no exception to this, as it is an expanding sector in India particularly in the wake of the opening of economy and the employees are likely to experience greater job-related strain caused by nature of work, higher authority, greater responsibilities and the kinds of subordinates.

In the light of these aspects, it seems relevant to focus on the work related stress faced by the bank employees, the stressors and their effects and the strategies for combating such stressors. In this context, the following questions arise:

1. What is the level of occupational stress faced by bank employees?
2. What are the factors influencing the occupational stress of the bank employees?

3. What are the sources of occupational stress to the bank employees?
4. To what extent, do the bank employees adopt coping strategies to reduce job stress?

## SCOPE OF THE STUDY

The present study focuses on the occupational stress in the banking sector. The study was designed to gain a better understanding of the factors that contribute to occupational stress experienced by the employees in this industry. The study also evaluates the stress management ability of the employees and the level of adoption of coping strategies.

## OBJECTIVES OF THE STUDY

The objectives of the study are:

1. To measure the level of occupational stress of bank employees.
2. To examine the factors influencing level of job stress.
3. To study the sources of occupational stress and analyse the influencing factors.
4. To identify the stressors which discriminate between employees of high stress and low stress.
5. To understand the relationship between individuals' "personality type" and their stress managing ability.
6. To study the effects of job stress on the individuals and the organisation.
7. To examine the significant stress coping strategies adopted by bank employees.
8. To analyse the relationship between demographic and job related variables and level of adoption of stress coping strategies.

## HYPOTHESES

The researcher has formulated and tested the following null hypotheses keeping in view the wider theoretical framework and objective two of the study:

1. There is no significant difference among employees belonging to different age groups as regards level of job stress.
2. There is no significant difference between employees belonging to the two gender groups with respect to level of job stress.
3. Employees' level of stress is independent of their marital status.
4. Differences in the level of education do not cause difference in the level of job stress.
5. There is no significant difference among employees belonging to different salary groups with respect to level of stress.
6. There is no significant difference between employees belonging to the two types of banks as regards level of job stress.
7. Level of job stress is independent of employees' nature of job.
8. There is no significant difference among employees having different periods of service with respect to level of stress.

To fulfil objective three of the study, the following null hypotheses were formulated and tested:

1. There is no significant difference among employees belonging to the different age groups with respect to stressors.
2. There is no significant difference between employees belonging to the two gender groups with respect to stressors.
3. There is no significant difference among employees belonging to the different educational levels with respect to stressors.
4. There is no significant difference among employees belonging to the different levels of salary with respect to stressors.

5. There is no significant difference between employees belonging to the two types of banks with respect to sources of stress.

6. There is no significant difference among employees of different designations with respect to stressors.

7. There is no significant difference among employees of different levels of experience with respect to stressors.

In line with the objective eight of the study, the following null hypotheses were formulated and tested:

1. There is no significant difference among employees belonging to the different age groups with respect to the level of adoption of coping strategies.

2. There is no significant difference between the employees belonging to the two gender groups with respect to the level of adoption of coping strategies.

3. There is no significant difference among bank employees belonging to different educational groups with respect to coping strategies.

4. There is no significant difference among employees earning different amounts of salary with respect to coping strategies.

5. There is no significant difference between the bank employees belonging to public sector and private sector banks with respect to various coping strategies.

6. There is no significant difference among employees having different nature of jobs with respect to coping strategies.

7. There is no significant difference among employees having different periods of service with respect to coping strategies.

## OPERATIONAL DEFINITIONS

Various stress related terms used in this study which are defined by well known authors are given as follows:

### Occupational Stress

'Occupational stress' is the interaction of the work conditions with the characteristics of the worker such that the demands of work exceed the ability of the worker to cope with them. (Randall, E). He opined that the presence of stress at work can also be called 'Job stress'. Hence in this study both these terms viz. 'Occupational stress' and 'Job Stress' are used synonymously.

### Stressor

The term 'stressor' refers to the specific causes/reasons for stress. It is the stimulus which induces stress. (Hans Selye).

### Role Overload

It is a situation in which employees feel that they are being asked to do more than time or ability permits (Sales and Heure).

### Role Conflict

When the behaviour expected of an individual by others in the organisation is inconsistent, he will be in a state of role conflict. (Khan, Sarbin and Miles)

### Role Ambiguity

This is a job situation in which there are inadequate or misleading pieces of information about how an individual is supposed to do the job. (Beehr)

### Job Difficulty

Kasl states that job difficulty is experienced when a job involves repetitiveness or demands continuous attention resulting in poor mental health of the individual.

### Role Stagnation

Role stagnation refers to fewer opportunities for learning and growth in the role.

## METHODOLOGY

### Sample Design

Multi-stage sampling has been used in the study.

### Selection of District

In the first stage, Erode District has been selected for convenience.

## Selection of Sample Bank Branches

The study has been confined to the employees of commercial banks located in Erode District, comprising of public sector and private sector banks. The researcher, in the second stage, identified the total number of branches of public sector and private sector banks in Erode District. The total number of bank branches in the district stood at 209 as on 31st March 2005. The details of the bank branches have been presented in Table 1.1

**Table – 1.1**

**Total Number of Bank Branches in Erode District as on 31st March 2005**

| *S. No.* | *Types of Banks* | *No. of branches* |
|---|---|---|
| 1. | Public Sector Banks | 144 |
| 2. | Private Sector Banks | 65 |
| | **Total** | **209** |

*Source:* Banking Statistics published by Lead bank Office, Canara Bank, Erode, 2004-05.

These 209 bank branches constituted the sample frame for the selection of banks. 20 per cent each, of the public sector banks and private sector banks were selected by using random sampling (by drawing lots) technique. Thus 42 bank branches were selected which consisted of 29 public sector and 13 private sector bank branches.

## Selection of Employees

The selected 29 public sector bank branches had totally 360 employees, out of whom 294 employees were selected for the study. Forty employees who were assistants were excluded along with another 26 employees who were unwilling to respond. Assistants were excluded because their nature of work is not comparable with the other employees.

There were totally 131 employees in the selected 13 private sector bank branches. Nineteen of them were assistants and 6 were not co-operative. So, they were excluded from the study. The remaining 106 employees were included in the sample.

The details of the sample covered by the study have been presented in Table – 1.2.

Table – 1.2

**Composition of Sample**

| *Types of Banks* | *No. of sample branches* | *No. of sample respondents* |
|---|---|---|
| Public Sector Banks | 29 | 294 |
| Private Sector Banks | 13 | 106 |
| **Total** | **42** | **400** |

### Data Source

The study was fully based on primary data. The tool constructed for the collection of data was a questionnaire for the sample employees of the selected bank branches.

Personal data pertaining to the employees were included in the first part (A) of the questionnaire. The other parts of the questionnaire were so designed as to get information regarding sources of stress and level of stress in Part B, identifying personality traits and measuring stress management ability in Part C and D respectively. Questions in Part E were designed to study the effect of job stress and that of Part F to understand the stress coping strategies.

### Pilot Study and Pre-Testing

A pilot study was conducted on 50 employees of public sector and private sector banks in order to check the validity of the questions and to understand the difficulties of the respondents in giving their responses. On the basis of the pilot study, the questionnaire was redesigned with suitable modifications.

### Quantification and Measurement of Variables and Construction of Scales

The objectives of the study included measuring the level of occupational stress of bank employees; identifying the factors causing occupational stress and understanding the relationship between personality traits and stress managing ability of bank employees. Studying the effects of job stress on the individuals and the organisation, examining the significant stress coping strategies adopted by bank employees and studying the relationship between demographic and job related variables and level of adoption of stress coping strategies were also included in the objectives.

To measure the level of job stress and to identify the sources of job stress, a five-point scale on the Likert Model has been constructed. In this scale, 30 statements relating to stress have been included. The scores awarded to the responses of positive statements [Questions B1, B2, B3 and B4] were, strongly agree-1, agree-2, neutral-3, disagree-4 and strongly disagree-5. The remaining statements were negative for which scores were awarded as, strongly agree-5, agree-4, neutral-3, disagree-2 and strongly disagree-1.

In order to understand the stress management ability of the bank employees, a three-point scale was constructed. 4 components were included in the construction of scale. For negative statements [Questions D1 and D3], scores awarded were, agree-1, neutral-2 and disagree-3. The remaining were positive statements [Questions D2 and D4] and were awarded scores as, agree-3, neutral-2 and disagree-1.

The effects of job stress of bank employees have been measured by the construction of another five-point scale with 9 statements. The scores awarded to negative statements were, strongly agree-5, agree-4, neutral-3, disagree-2 and strongly disagree-1, i.e., for statements E1, E2, E3, E4, E6 and E7. The remaining statements being positive, scores awarded were, strongly agree-1, agree-2, neutral-3, disagree-4 and strongly disagree-5.

The level of adoption of stress coping strategies by the bank employees has been measured by constructing a scale with 24 components. This scale has been designed as a three-point scale. The scores awarded for each of the components were, never-1, sometimes-2 and always-3.

The relationship of demographic variables and job related variables on job stress has also been studied. Those variables were:

**Demographic Variables**

1. Age;
2. Gender;
3. Marital Status;
4. Educational Qualification; and
5. Total monthly emoluments.

**Job Related Variables**

1. Nature of job;
2. Type of bank; and
3. Length of service.

## FRAMEWORK OF ANALYSIS

The analysis and tabulation of results were performed by the use of the statistical analysis package, Statistical Package for Social Sciences (SPSS). Statistical tools such as Descriptive Statistics, Factor Analysis, Discriminant Function Analysis, Weighted average, Correlation and Analysis of Variance were used in the study.

For the purpose of the first and second objectives, i.e., to measure the level of job stress of bank employees and to examine the factors influencing level of job stress, descriptive statistics and chi-square analysis have been applied.

Factor analyses have been employed to fulfil the third objective of identifying the sources of job stress and the seventh objective, viz., examining the significant stress coping strategies adopted by bank employees.

Discriminant function analysis has been performed to identify the stressors which discriminate between employees of high stress and low stress.

Weighted average analysis has been employed to study the effects of job stress on the employees and on the bank. The same tool has also been applied to ascertain the most effective coping strategies adopted by bank employees.

Analysis of variance has been used to study the relationship between demographic and job related variables and level of adoption of stress coping strategies and also to study whether the stressors differ according to differences in the demographic and job related variables.

As regards the fifth objective, i.e., to understand the relationship between personality type and stress management ability of bank employees, correlation analysis has been used.

## LIMITATIONS OF THE STUDY

1. Non occupational stressors have not been considered in the present study as they did not come under the purview of the present study.
2. The responses and attitude of respondents may differ from time to time. This is an inherent limitation in all the researches on behavioural sciences.
3. Co-operative banks are excluded from this study.
4. Physical factors such as lighting, ventilation and noise were not considered in the analysis relating to stressors.

## ORGANISATIONS OF THE STUDY

Organisation of the study is as follows:

The first chapter consists of the introduction and design of the study, comprising of statement of the problem, scope of the study, objectives, methodology, limitations and chapter scheme.

The second chapter deals with the review of related literature. It has been presented as literature relating to causes, literature relating to effects and those relating to the coping strategies.

The third chapter focuses on the stress management strategies at the organisational level.

Statistical analyses and interpretations relating to the level of stress, causes of stress, effects of stress, personality type and stress management ability and coping strategies are presented in the fourth chapter.

The fifth chapter recapitulates the key findings of the study and offers suitable suggestions.

# Chapter–2

# REVIEW OF PREVIOUS STUDIES

## INTRODUCTION

Employing and retaining staff is a huge investment for an organisation. Globalisation and Information Technology are currently transforming the Indian banking radically. Innovation has brought out new banking products and services which have resulted in heavy competition between banks. So employees have to cope with the work pressure which leads to more of mental stress than physical strain. There has been continuous research in the areas of employee stress, stress coping strategies and its impact on work. Hence empirical studies relating to job stress, effect of stress and coping strategies are reviewed, which proved to be very useful to the researcher in getting an insight into the main objectives of the study and finalising the methodology.

A brief account of review of previous studies is presented in this chapter.

**Studies related to causes of job stress are being reviewed here.**

**a. Review of studies relating to job stress of bank employees**

*Bhatnagar D and Bore K (1985)* studied, "Organisational role stresses among branch managers" of a banking organisation and found that respondents do not really experience major stress in the areas of role ambiguity, role stagnation and staff-role distance. However, this study analysed the stress among the bank branch managers only, without considering the other employees[1].

*Rajeshwari T.R. (1992)* conducted a research work entitled "Employee Stress: A study with reference to bank employees" with a sample of 34 officers and 79 clerks from five nationalised banks. The study revealed structural rigidity and poor physical working conditions as sources of stress". This study failed to indicate the coping strategies followed to reduce job stress[2].

*Chand and Sethi (1997)* found in a study on 150 junior management officers in banks, that there is a significant positive relationship between job-related strain and role overload and role conflict. Factors such as role ambiguity, under-participation and responsibility also predicted role stress though not significantly according to this study[3].

This study however has been undertaken to study the organisational factors of stress only. The factors such as individual factors, physical factors, extra-organisational factors have not been considered.

In a study 'Employee occupational stress in banking' conducted by *Michailidis M and Georgiou Y (2006),* a sample of 60 bank employees at different organisational levels and educational backgrounds was used. Data collection utilised the Occupational Stress Indicator (OSI). Results of data analysis provided evidence that employees' educational levels affect the degree of stress they experience in various ways. However, this study did not analyse the stress coping strategies to be followed by the bank employees[4].

**b. Review of Studies Relating to Job Stress in General**

*Kahn et al (1964)* in their study on "Organisational stress: Studies in Role conflict and Ambiguity" identified role conflict with one of the forms of role based stress, with the absence of role ambiguity[5].

In his study on "Integrating the Individual and the Organisation", *Argyris C (1964)* has pointed out that job related tension and job dissatisfaction are correlated with little participation in decision making, ambiguity about job security and poor use of skills and abilities[6].

*Caplan et al., (1975)* have identified the lack of participation in the decision making process, lack of effective consultation and communication, unjustified restrictions on behaviour, office politics and no sense of belonging as potential sources of stress. The study concluded that lack of participation in work activity is associated with negative psychological mood and behavioural responses, including escapist drinking and heavy smoking[7].

"Stress and Work", a research study undertaken by *Ivencevich, JM and Matterson MT (1980)* identified three critical factors such as role ambiguity, role conflict and the degree of responsibility as the major sources of employees' stress. This study did promote some understanding about stressors but did not provide realistic solutions to reduce the effect of job stress[8].

In *1980, Natha* showed that role conflict is experienced more frequently at the middle management rather than at the lower management level; supervisors manifest relatively higher role conflict than managers, whereas both managers and supervisors manifest higher role conflict than workers. This study also demonstrated that role conflict decreases with an increase in job tenure in an organisation[9].

*Srivastava A K and Singh A P (1981),* in their study on "Construction and standardisation of occupational stress index: A pilot study", have developed an occupational stress index. It assesses perceived occupational stress related to role overload, role ambiguity, role conflict, group and political pressures, responsibility for persons, under participation, powerlessness, poor peer relations, intrinsic impoverishment, low status, strenuous working conditions and unprofitability[10].

"Organisational Determinants of Anxiety based Management Stress", a study conducted by *Das G S (1982)* reported that negative work group climate and powerlessness may be dominant cause of stress experienced by Indian managers than role ambiguity[11].

According to *Narayanan's (1983)* study, "Role Conflict Differential (RCD): A direct method of assessing the role conflict", over load, difficulty in the task domain, the demands and the requirements are closely associated with role conflict[12].

In a Meta analysis, *Jackson and Schuler (1985),* on role ambiguity and role conflict, found no relationship between role stress variables and individual characteristics. With respect to age, they felt that there were no theoretical reasons to predict that age should be correlated with role ambiguity or role conflict, though spurious correlation may occur due to an association of age with job experience or tenure[13].

"A study of stress among executives" done by *Ahmad S, Bharadwaj A and Narula S (1985)* found that public sector executives experience slightly more stress than their counterparts in the private sector. Background factors like age, education, income, experience and marital status of executives were unrelated to role stress in both the groups[14].

*Baroudi J J and Ginzberg M J (1986)* in their study, "Impact of Technological Environment on Programmers/ Analysts Job outcomes", showed that the work of software professionals is a team based one that requires them to function from different locations as a part of a functional team as well as report to several people at various levels. This causes software professionals to receive conflicting job performance information and hence there is a lack of clear and precise information about what is expected of them[15].

*Sandhimann (1988),* in his research work stated that employees who are under increasing pressure to appear enthusiastic, interested, cheerful and friendly at all times in their work place are highly stressed[16].

The main findings of *Kumar S (1989),* in his "Study of Role Stress, Role Satisfaction and Role Efficacy among public sector executives" indicated that unmarried executives, executives married to working women and marketing executives married have significantly higher total role stress. Role stagnation and personal adequacy were found to be significantly higher among lower level executives[17].

"Are you killing yourself", a research paper by *Dastur R H (1990)* states that work group climate is an important cause of managerial stress and perceived power is the second most potent cause of managerial stress. Role ambiguity did not arise as a significant cause of stress in this study. Thus, negative group climate and powerlessness may be dominant causes of stress experienced by Indian managers[18].

From the findings of his study *Cummins, R (1990),* suggested role conflict and ambiguity, work overload, under utilisation of skills, resource inadequacy and lack of participation as the main categories of work stressors[19].

*McDonald and Korabik (1991)* in their study titled "Sources of stress and ways of coping among male and female managers" studied stress and coping among managers. Ten male managers in a low stress group and ten male and ten female managers in a high stress group described stressful work-related situations that they had experienced, and how they coped with them. A work stress questionnaire was used to assess additional type of stressors. It was found that women were more likely than men to report that prejudice and discrimination and work/family interferences were sources of stress[20].

A study on "Stress and strain among Indian Middle Managers" has been made by *Singh AP and Singh B (1992).* They asked 400 middle-level managers of Bokaro Steel Plant to fill out role stress and job anxiety questionnaires. Their result showed that high anxiety employees showed positive relationship with role stress[21].

*Singh A (1993),* in his work, "Stress in newspaper industry", explained that research evidence suggests certain kinds of professions/occupations cause greater stress than others. For example, Singh found technocrats to experience greater stress in their job when compared to non-technocrats[22].

*Biswas U N (1998)* studied the relationship between "life style stressors and organisational effectiveness'. He collected data from 160 managers, 47 supervisors and 50 workers of public sector organisation. His results showed that the stress caused by performance, threat and frustration led to low degree of organisational commitment[23].

"Occupational stress among Information Technology Personnel in Singapore" – A study by *Lim and Alan (1999)* analysed the factors which generated stress among information personnel in Singapore. Lack of career advancement, workload, risk-taking and decision making and employee morale and organisational culture were identified as four broad categories of stressors[24].

A study by *Vijayalakshmi and Meti V (2000),* found that non-executive employees exhibited signs of significantly higher occupational stress than executives on such dimensions as role conflict, political pressure, poor peer relations and job responsibility[25].

*Patnayak B (2000),* in his study, "Effect of shift work and hierarchical position in satisfaction commitment stress and HR climate", found that the level of stress experienced does not vary by position. Executives and supervisors irrespective of the shift did not show significant differences in their job stress[26].

*Mishra PK and Rani DL (2001)* conducted a study on "Occupational stress among women in emerging services". They collected data on 39 young and 23 old doctors as well as 50 young and 32 old nurses. Their results show that while older doctors and nurses experienced more role stagnation they found their job less stressful. On the other hand, young doctors and nurses felt greater personal inadequacy and hence experienced greater stress at work[27].

*Adguide.com (2001),* conducted a survey on 1400 chief information officers working in U.S companies. Rising workload, office politics, work life balance issues, commuting and pace of technology were reported as stressors[28].

*K.S. Rajeswari and R.N. Anantharaman (2003),* in their study on "Role of need for clarity in the relation between occupational stress and work exhaustion among software professionals" explored the role of need-for-clarity in the relationship between occupational stress and work exhaustion among software professionals in India. The study was based on 156 responses obtained from software industry in India. They found that need-for-clarity served to moderate the relationship between stress caused by threat of obsolescence, work family interface and technical constraints and work exhaustion[29].

*Zvid. Gellis, Jongchun Kim, Sung Chul Hwang (2004)* in their study entitled "New York state care Manager Survey: urban and rural difference in job activities, job stress and job satisfaction" made research to study the quality of working life of care managers in urban and rural community mental health programmes in New York state. The objectives were to describe specific job activities and examine differences in the perceptions of job stress and job satisfaction. Urban care managers attributed greater job stress intensity and frequency than did rural workers to stressors relating to collaborating and coordinating services. Urban care managers reported higher levels of perceived job stress due to organisational support deficits than did rural workers[30].

However these studies did little to view the sources or causes of occupational stress as they have not analysed the factors in detail.

**Studies with respect to effects of job stress are detailed below:**

**a. Review of Studies Relating to Effects of Stress of Bank Employees**

*Osipow, et al (1985)* in their study of occupational stress found no significant effect on the quality of work on the bank employees[31].

In a report released Christchurch *coroner* found that work stress was the main factor behind the suicide of an Australia and New Zealand (ANZ) Bank worker. The report pointed out the effect of stress among employees of Australia and New Zealand Bank only[32].

**b. Review of Studies Relating to Effects of Stress in General**

*Keniston (1965),* in his study on "The uncommitted: alienated youth in American Society", has explained that alienated individuals often appear to be angry and depressive. In the early stage of burnout, individuals experience perceptual feelings of anger. When a calm, accepting and easy going individual begins to burnout he becomes chronically angry. Individual's anger often becomes more focussed if the work stress of the individuals is unabated, the study concluded[33].

The findings of the study, "Reactions to a Study of Bureaucracy and Alienation" done by *Anderson B O (1971)*, emphasised that when an individual perceives to have lost his/her control over his/her self and is constrained to act according to the forces external to him/her, he/she feels alienated. Alienation is no longer confined to worker and all sections of personal experience alienation under condition just cited[34].

*Freudenberger (1977)* has examined the effect of stress in his study on "Burnout: The occupational hazard of the child care worker". He has concluded in his study that the stress experienced by child care worker is found to increase fatigue and turn the individual cynical and left with burnout[35].

If the individual experiences job stress for any period of time, he or she likely becomes demoralised and he or she is ineffective in problem solving, according to *Lazarus & Launier (1978)* in their study on "Stress-related transactions between person and environment"[36].

The findings of the study, "Burned-out Cops and their families" made by *Maslach C & Jackson S.E. (1979)* pointed out that burnout people lose interest in their job and develop intentions to leave their job[37].

Thomas *G Cummings and Gary L Cooper (1979)* in their study, A Cybernetic Framework for studying occupational stress" analysed the impact of job stress on the employees' physical health. However, this study could not throw light on the impact of job stress of employees on their work[38].

It may also be argued that job stress is not always negative. Low levels of stress can enhance employee's motivation and job performance. However, *Cherniss (1980)* in his study "Staff Burnout: Job stress in the Human Services" argues that psychological stress is more disruptive than motivating the workers if the job stress reaches high levels. The disruptive nature of the stress depends on the complexity of task[39].

According to *Chermiss, C. (1980)* in his book, "Staff burnout: "Job stress in human service, studies on burnout found that, it is related to exhaustion and work over load factors in various organisations (Green and Walkey, 1988; Chermiss, 1980; Freudenberger, 1977, 1980). Stress on the job according to the author is costly for employers, which is reflected in lower productivity, reduced motivation and job skills, and increased and accidents[40].

The study on "The work stress connection: How to cope with job burnout" made by *Veninga, R.L., & Sparadley, J.P., (1981)* revealed that the individual who perceives stress higher will find less relief and burnout more easily; on the other hand the individual who perceives stress lower will find less risk. Perception of tension with regard to family pressures, environmental demands and work problems are two major stress points for many individuals. If these factors are not controlled, the risk factors can undermine one's health and well-being[41].

In a study of 170 bank employees, consisting of 70 officers and 100 clerks conducted by *Devi S R (1982)* entitled "A study of Role conflict in relation to anxiety, alienation and probabilistic orientation", it is revealed that probabilistic orientation does not have significant effect on role conflict[42].

*Singh A P and Singh H C (1984),* in their study on "Occupational stress, security-insecurity and job involvement of first level industrial supervisors", investigated the influence of occupational stress and security-insecurity on job involvement of first level industrial supervisors. The findings showed significant positive relationship between occupational stress and job involvement[43].

A study of 134 elementary regular and special education teachers by *Holt (1985)* titled "A study of the interaction levels of occupational stress, degree of burnout and personality hardiness in female elementary teachers" revealed that those who had high levels of occupational stress and a low level of burnout felt less alienated and those with high levels of occupational stress and a high level of burnout felt more alienated. The findings also suggest that alienation was significantly correlated with levels of stress, emotional exhaustion and physical illness[44].

In the study on "Role of social support in the experience of stress at work", *Daniel C, Ganster and Bronston T Mayes, (1986)* have examined the role of social support in the experience of work stress. The results indicated that social support shows a consistent relation with a variety of stress outcomes[45].

*Pestonjee D M (1987),* in his study on "Executive stress" should it be avoided?" revealed that managers and systems analysts in private organisations have more stress and satisfaction when compared with their counterparts in public organisations[46].

The study conducted by *Whitehead, J.T. (1987)* on "Probation Officer job burnout: A test if Two Theories" revealed that stress and burnout are not synonymous, rather excessive and prolonged levels of job stress produce strain and result in burnout on the part of the individual if the coping mechanism adopted by the individual is improper[47].

*Chatterjee A (1992),* in his study on Commitment cognitive appraisal and occupational stress, conducted the study on 300 technical personnel at the middle level of management in the heavy engineering industry. On the basis of their score on self efficacy they were divided into the high and low efficacy categories. When their occupational stress score was compared, high efficacy employees experienced greater occupational stress than their low efficacy counterparts[48].

In the study on "Men and women in transitional pattern of stress strain and social relations", *Singh AL and Sehgal P (1995)* have explained that gender and age difference also contribute to differences in the experiences of stress. Singh and Sehgal collected data on 172 respondents. Their results showed that though male and female do not differ on various dimensions of stress, male respondents showed greater somatic problems while female respondents were characterised by greater anxiety[49].

"Job stress, satisfaction and mental health: An empirical examination of self-employed and non-self employed Canadians" – a research study conducted by *Mohammad Jamal (1997)* had examined the differences between full time self employed and organisationally employed Canadians in a large metropolitan city on the East Coast with regard to their work and non work experiences. From the analysis of data collected, he found the self employed experienced higher job stress, non work satisfaction and psychosomatic health problems and spent more time in voluntary organisations than non self employed[50].

*HansBosma, Richard Peter, Johannes Siegrist and Michael Marmot (1998)* in their work on "Two alternative job stress models and the risk of Coronary Heart Disease", examined the association between two alternative job stress models – the effort reward imbalance model and the job strain model – and the risk of Coronary heart disease among male and female British civil servants. The findings of the study indicated that the imbalance between personal efforts (competitiveness, work-related over-commitment and hostility) and rewards (poor promotion prospectus and a blocked career) was associated with a higher risk of new coronary heart disease[51].

In the study on "Stress in Managers and Professionals in Indian organisations", *Ashok K Sahni (1998),* revealed that low stressed group compared with the high stressed group tends to be significantly higher in respect of their job commitment, self esteem, satisfaction and good human relations. According to the researchers, they were more flexible in their attitudes and values and experience lesser conflict with their superiors[52].

In his research work entitled, "A study of relationship between personality dimensions and organisational role stress in a public sector organisation", *Pandey C.S. (1998)* wanted to study the personality predisposition and its impact on the experience of stress. He collected data from 450 employees of BHEL (150 senior managers, 150 junior managers and 150 supervisors). His results showed that Psychoticism – reality, neuroticism – stability dimensions of personality were found to be associated with higher levels of stress. On the other hand extroversion – introversion was negatively correlated with perceived organisational stress[53].

In his study on "Job Stress and Employees", *Luolu (1999)* has investigated the relationship between occupational stressors (job demands, discretion and interpersonal conflicts) and strain (job satisfaction and mental health); and impact of two potential moderating variables; work motivation (intrinsic versus extrinsic) and social support from colleagues, superiors, friends and families. 300 working adults were interviewed. Intrinsic work motivation was positively related to overall job satisfaction, whereas extrinsic motivation was positively related to depression; both supervisor's support and family support were negatively related to depression, anxiety and somatic symptoms, the study concluded[54].

*Mishra PK and Rani DL (2001)* in their study on Occupational Stress among working women in emerging services, collected data from 144 doctors and 82 nurses drawn from various hospitals. Their results show that nurses experience greater stress in their job as compared to doctors[55].

*Cleopatra A Veloustson and George G Panigyaraksib (2004)*, in their work, "Consumer Brand Managers' job stress, job satisfaction, perceived performance and intention leave", examined the effect of brand managers' role stress (role ambiguity, role conflict and role overload) perceived performance and satisfaction on the intention to leave. The results revealed that increased role stress is associated with lower levels of perceived job performance and job satisfaction, but its influence on the intention to leave was not significant. In addition, higher levels of perceived job performance and lower levels of satisfaction were generally associated with higher intention to leave[56].

*Andrew Marantz (2006)* in his article "U. Mississippi: Editorial: Stress management more important than ever" stated that common reactions to stress include eating or avoiding food, smoking, pacing, drinking or having emotional breakdowns. These were often signs that stress levels had built to an unhealthy level as per the analysis made in this study. The author suggested developing positive attitudes, finding a friend or mentor who would listen to one's problems on a regular basis to deal with the stress in a healthier fashion[57].

This study failed to understand the effects of occupational stress as they have paid least attention to the individual reactions to the stressful events and outcomes of such experiences.

**Studies with respect to coping strategies are detailed below:**

**a. Review of Studies Relating to Coping Strategies followed by Bank Employees**

*Sen (1987)* studied the personal and organisational correlates to role stress and coping strategies among bank employees. The defensive style of coping was found to be the most common, followed by the "introspective" style and then the "imperative" style. No sex differences were found in coping styles. A tendency was found for those with higher income to solve problems by their own efforts, probably because of the power and authority conferred by higher paying positions. However, this study did not analyse the relationship between demographic variables and level of coping strategies[58].

Coping strategies reported by *Saranya A.S. (1999)* in her study 'Job stress of Bank Employees' as adopted by bank employees were relaxation techniques, utilisation of home resources, distraction techniques and rational task oriented behaviour[59].

*Howard, et al (1975)* found in a study of 300 bank managers that the coping strategies were effective for all the age groups[60].

**b. Review of Studies Relating to Coping Strategies in Various Organisations**

*James C Quick and Janathen D Quick (1979)* in their work "Reducing stress through preventive management" concluded that organisational techniques like Role Analysis Technique (RAT), work redesign, job enrichment, performance planning and individual techniques like aerobic exercise, relaxation response and psychotherapy are preventive techniques which would to improve quality of work life and also individual and organisational effectiveness[61].

*Singh (1982)* undertook a study to ascertain the psychological correlates of role stress and coping styles for working women. Singh found that professional women most often used the "defensive" style to cope with stress, and that the differential and avoidance styles were used twice as often as functional styles. Women entrepreneurs used the approach oriented style more than the professional women as per the findings of the study[62].

*Gupta and Murthy (1984),* in their work entitled "Role conflict and coping strategies – a study on Indian women" studied role conflict and coping strategies among Indian women. Their qualitative data indicated that "adjustment" and "compromise" were the most commonly used and successful methods of coping[63].

*Caplan, Naidu and Tripathi (1984),* in their work, "Coping and defence" examined how patterns of coping and defence as well as their main effects influence well-being. They suggested that coping may buffer the effects of stressors on well-being only when stressors are subjectively controllable[64].

*Singh and Sinha (1985)* in their research "Relationship of coping strategies with job related strain" studied the relationship of coping strategies with job related strain among 156 male supervisory level executives of a large industrial organisation, using a measure of coping strategy designed by the researchers themselves. They found that various dimensions of coping strategies were related to strain dimensions in a specific pattern of weighted linear combination. Considered individually, they found that cheerful and optimistic work orientation and yogic resources appeared to be superior cooping strategies[65].

*Tandon (1986),* in his research work titled, "Development of a measure of stress tolerance" hypothesised that those who cope with life like stresses without impairing their health would be characterised by a more positive philosophy of life and perception of meaning even while suffering. She administered an 85-item stress scale to 540 employees. The group which, reported few symptoms was designated the superior health group. It was found that the superior health subjects and a positive self image, thought well of others, perceived a positive meaning in suffering and believed that prayers helped[66].

*Susan McCammon et al (1987),* have evolved in their study, "Managing workplace stress" that the most frequently endorsed coping strategies following both events involved attempts to reach cognitive mastery over the event and to ascertain meaning. Strategies of alerting activities and finding new interests were not frequently endorsed. A greater number of coping responses were endorsed following the tornado along with strategies which involved seeking support from others. Factor analysis of coping inventory responses revealed four factors: seeking of meaning, regaining mastery through individual action, regaining mastery through interpersonal action and philosophical self-contemplation[67].

"Role stress, locus of control, coping styles and role efficacy: A study of first generation entrepreneurs", by *Gupta (1989)* analysed organisational role stress and coping strategies among public sectors with specific objective of relating these to length of service in the organisation. Pareek's "ORS" scale was used to assess role and "Role Pics" used to assess the coping style. Gupta found that "avoidance" coping style was used by 69 per cent of the executives to cope with stress[68].

In a study, "Appraisal of stress and coping in college students", *Mehta (1989),* used two specific stressful events and a measure of appraisal of the events as well as a coping checklist to study appraisal and coping among 258 college students. He found more similarities than differences in the styles of coping across situations. Coping styles were found to differ in relation to appraisal. Challenge appraisal in both academic and personal situations was related to the use of problem solving methods of coping and positive thinking as per this study[69].

The study on "Coping among dual-career men and women across the family life cycle" made by *Maureen H. Schnittger, Gloria W Bird (1990),* indicates that differences in coping across five family life cycle stages are identified using responses from 329 dual career women and men. Coping strategy use differs significantly by gender and life cycle stage. Women utilise the coping strategies of Cognitive, Restructuring, Delegating, Limiting Advocational Activities, and using social support significantly more often than do men. Dual career men and women without children at home use compartmentalising significantly less frequently than men and women with children, the study concluded[70].

*Singh (1990)* in his thesis on "Coping strategies as moderator of the relationship between organisational role stress and mental health" studied strategies as a moderator of the relationship between organisational role stress and mental health on a sample of 300 employees of a supervisory cadre from the Life Insurance Corporation of India. It was found in this study that the use of "avoidance" coping strategy enhanced mental ill health while the "approach" coping strategy attenuated the severity of mental ill health[71].

"Coping with job stress: which strategies work best?" by *Gary F Korske, Stuart A Kirk and Randi D Koeshe (1993),* in a four-wave panel study the coping styles of care managers hired to work with seriously and persistently mentally ill clients ere measured at entry to the job. Depending on time period and outcome variable studied, the effect of coping was examined in between 39 and 51 workers. The results showed that control-oriented coping strategies clearly acted as work stress buffers and that those who relied exclusively on avoidance coping strategies reported higher general levels of negative consequences three months later[72].

*Ray, Eilen Berlin and Miller, Katherine I (1994)* in their study titled, "Social Support: Home/work stress and burnout; who can help?" have found that home-work conflict is a source of stress for women in human service occupations and proved that social support from intra-organisational and extra-organisational sources would help individuals from such stress[73].

*Ahmed, Bhatt and Ahmad (1998),* in a study titled "Stress and coping strategies among executives technocrats" found that men preferred a defensive style more often than women. They found no relationship for age, number of dependants, income, drinking/smoking habits, and health with the strategies used for coping with stress[74].

*Sanders D (1999)* conducted research on "Post office counters stress". The recommendations of the study for managing stress include organisation-wide initiatives, development of employee health services, job design and restructuring and individual skill development[75].

The study on "Customer stress – relaxation: the impact of music in a hospital waiting room" conducted by *Tansik D A & Routhieaux R (1999)* concluded that music in the waiting room had a significant effect on reducing visitor stress. This experiment is considered to be a low cost way of improving the quality of life of customers[76].

According to the findings of the study, "Learning the Tao of meditation training by *Luthar H K (1999),* meditation is form of stress relaxation for employees. It is claimed that this form of training can lower health care costs, reduce job-related and psychological stress, reduce absenteeism, and keep workers rejuvenated[77].

*Briner R (2000),* in his study on "Stress Management: Effectiveness of interventions" has identified seven interventions as stress management techniques. They are stress management training, employee assistance programmes, job redesign, stress audits, risk management, improvement in health and fitness and the establishment of standard management practices[78].

The study on "When stress won't go away" conducted by *Atkison W (2000)* showed that in many jobs, stress is unavoidable and inevitable, and employees tend to cope with it and react to it in different ways. Some enjoy the challenge of stress in their work. It is argued, therefore, that activities that are focussed on reducing stress in the workplace can sometimes be more harmful than helpful. Employers need to ensure that the right employees are chosen to fill the jobs where stress is inherent. Employees also have to take responsibility of identifying the jobs that they will enjoy doing. The important role for manager is to help employees become more resilient to stress, especially in a crisis. These were the main conclusions of this study[79].

A research has been conducted by *Cristallini V (2000)* on "Stress and the improvement of working conditions: an individual and collective responsibility". The research was conducted in various departments of a large French hospital, a residential centre for handicapped adults and a help centre for unemployed people. The findings of the study indicated that stress was an integral part of the manager's workload. Stress could be treated by organising and improving the serenity of the person and his activities which could be done through a programme of activity management methods, with the advantage of not necessarily impinging directly on the psychology of the individual nor on the group dynamic[80].

*Yandrick R M (2000)* has examined the coping techniques in his work, "Getting by with a little help from friends". According to him, many employers have employees were reluctant to receive help for their behavioural problems. The researcher stated that one way in which employers were addressing such problem behaviours was through the provision of peer-to-peer assistance[81].

The study on "Counselling: a primary stress intervention" made by *Hill C (2000)* suggests that the function of workplace counselling within the organisational culture is helpful in reducing the stress[82].

According to the study on "Managing the pressure" conducted by *Harrington T (2000)* the approach to managing the pressure included learn and share exercises, as well as the early location of individual stress through its human resource practices[83].

The findings of the study conducted by *Wah L (2000)* on "The emotional tightrope" indicated programmes to reduce employee stress to include sabbaticals, appointing toxic healers, or emotional healers to shoulder the burdens of intra-organisational emotional stress[84].

*Shailendra Singh and Arvind C Sinha (2002)* in their study "Empirical dimensions of strategies of coping with job related stress", identified three categories of coping strategies, namely, strategies which act on the source of stress, strategies which act on the symptomatic effects of stress and that which acts as an escape from the source and effects of stress[85].

In the study on "Emotional Intelligence and the bottom line; stress in the super market", *Wustemann L (2002)* has stated that the training increased levels of morale and the quality of working life and marginally lowered stress levels[86].

*Anna West (2006)* in his study, "Management: Stress: coping strategies for employers, explained that since stress was very often caused by how a person copes in the job, rather than the job itself, it was important to make sure that at the recruitment stage an individual's skills are accurately matched to the demands of the job. The study suggested training during employment and increasing the control, an employee has, over the work may help to reduce stress[8'].

## CONCLUSION

Review of related literature in the area of occupational stress experienced by employees of banks and other types of organisations has been made by the researcher to establish the validity of the research topic "Occupational Stress of Bank Employees". Various research studies made by eminent persons for a span of two decades in the areas of sources of stress, effects of job stress and coping strategies have been reviewed and the researcher has understood the gaps in the earlier studies and hence the present study has been carried out.

## REFERENCES

1. Bhatnagar D and Bose K (1985), Organisational Role Stress and Branch Managers, *Prajnan: Journal of Social and Management Sciences*, XIV (4), Oct-Dec, 349-360.

2. Rajeshwari T.R. (1992), Employee Stress: A Study with Reference to Bank Employees, *Indian Journal of Industrial Relations* [27(4), 419-429].

3. Chand P and Sethi AS (1997), Organisational Factors in Development of Work Stress. *Indian Journal of Industrial Relations* [32(4), pp 453-462].

4. http://www.ncbi.nlm.nih.gov/entrez

5. Kahn, R.L., Wolfe, D.M., Quinn, R.P., Snoek, J.D & Rosenthal R.A. (1964), *Organisational Stress: Studies in Role Conflict and Ambiguity*, New York, Wiely.

6. Argyris, C. (1964): Integrating the Individual and the Organisation. New York: Wiley.

7. Caplan, Naidu and Tripathi(1984), Coping and Defence: Constellations v/s. Components, *Journal of Health and Social Behaviour*, [25, pp. 303-320].

8. Ivancerich IM and Matterson MT (1980) *Stress and Work Glen View*, IL: Scott, Foreman.

9. Natha (1980), *Managing Stress*, New York: AMACOM.

10. Srivatsava, AK and Singh AP (1981), Construction and Standardisation of and Occupational Stress index: A Pilot Study, *Indian Journal of Clinical Psychology*, [8(2), 133-136].

11. Das GS (1982), Organisational Determinants of Anxiety Based Management Stress, *Vikalpa* [7(3), 217-222].

12. Narayanan, S., (1983): Role Conflict Differential (RCD): A Direct Method of Assessing the Role Conflict. *Unpublished Research Paper*, Bharathiar University, Coimbatore.

13. Jackson and Schuler (1985), A Meta Analysis and Conceptual Critique of Research on Role Ambiguity and Role Conflict in Work Settings, *Organisational Behaviour and Human Decision Processes*, 3 6 , pp. 16-18.

14. Ahmad S, Bharadwaj A and Naurala S (1985), A Study of Stress Among Executives, *Journal of Personality and Clinical Studies* [1(2), pp. 47-50].

15. Baroudi JJ and Ginzberg MJ (1986), Impact of Technological Environment on Programmer/Analysts Job Outcomes, *Communications of the ICM*, [29, 546-555].

16. Sandiman, *Research Psychologist*, University of Salford, (1998).

17. Kumar S (1989), A Study of Role Stress, Role Satisfaction and Role Efficacy Among Public Sector Executives, Ph.D. Thesis, MD University, Rohtak.

18. Dastur RH, (1990), Are you Killing Yourself, Mr. Executive, IBH Publishing House, Bombay.

19. Cummins R (1990), Job Stress and the Buffering Effect of Supervisory Support, *Group and Organisational Studies*, [15, 92-104].

20. McDonald and Korabik (1991), Sources of Stress and Ways of Coping Among Male and Female Managers, Special Issue: Hand Book on Job Stress, *Journal of Social Behaviour and Personality* [6(7), 185-198].

21. Singh AP and Singh B (1992), Stress and Strain Among Indian Middle Managers, *Indian Journal of Industrial Relations* [28(1), 71-84].

22. Singh A (1993), Stress in Newspaper Industry, *Journal of the Indian Academy of Applied Psychology*, [19, 69-75].

23. Biswas, UN (1998), Life Style Stressors, Organisational Commitment, Job Involvement, and Perceived Organisational Effectiveness Across Job Levels, *Indian Journal of Industrial Relations*, [34(3), 55-72].

24. Lim VKG and Hian TTS (1999), Occupational Stress Among Information Technology Personnel in Singapore, www. Occuphealth.file/info/asian/ap199/Singapore.

25. Vijaylaxmi AA and Meti V (2000), A Study of Occupational Stress Executives and Non-executives of Private Industrial Organisation, *Organisation Management*, [15(4), 26-32].

26. Pattanayak B, (2000), Effect of Shift Work and Hierarchical Position in Satisfaction Commitment Stress and HR Climate, *Management and Labour Studies* [25(2), 126-135].

27. Mishra PK and Rani DL (2001), Occupational Stress Among Working Women in Emerging Services, *Management and Labour Studies* [26(1), 25-36].

28. www.adguide.com (2001).

29. Rajeswari KS and Anantharaman RN (2003), Role of Need for Clarity in the Relation Between Occupational Stress and Work Exhaustion Among Software Professionals, *Management and Change*, Volume 7, Number 2, 2003.

30. Zvid Gellis, Jongchun Kim, Sung Chuk Hwang, New York State Care Manager Survey: Urban and Rural Differences in Job Activities, Job Stress, and Job Satisfaction, *The Journal of Behavioural Health Services and Research*, Oct.-Dec., 2004.

31. Osipow, S.H., Doty, R.E., and Spokane A.R. (1985), Occupational Stress, Strain a Coping Across the Life Span, *Journal of Vocational Behaviour*, 27, pp. 99-108.

32. http://www.wsws.org/articles

33. Keniston., (1965), The Uncommitted: Alienated Youth in American Society, New York: Dell.

34. Anderson, B.O (1971): Reactions to a Study of Bureacracy and Alienation. *Social Force*, 49, June, 614-621.

35. Freudenberger, H.J., (1977): Burnout: The Occupational Hazard of the Child Care Worker, *Child Care Quarterly*, Vol. 6, No. 2, pp. 90-99.

36. Lazarus, R.S. & Launier, R(1978): Stress-Related Transactions Between Person and Environment. In L.A. Pervin & M. Lewis (Eds.), *Internal and External Determinants of Behaviour*, New York: Plenum.

37. Maslach, C., & Jackson, S.E., (1979): Burned-out Cops and Their Families, *Psychology Today*, [12(12), 59-62].

38. Thomas G. Cummings and Cary L. Cooper, "A Lybernatic Framework for Studying Occupation Stress", *Human Relations*, May 1979, pp. 395-418.

39. Cherniss, C. (1980); *Staff Burnout: Job Stress in the Human Services*. Beverly Hills, CA: Sage.

40. ibid.

41. Veninga, R.L., & Spradley, J.P., (1981): *The Work Stress Connection: How to Cope with Job Burnout*, Boston: Little Brown and Company.

42. Devi, S.R., (1982): A Study of Role Conflict in Relation to Anxiety, Alienation and Probabilistic Orientation. *Unpublished M.Phil. Dissertation*, University of Madras.

43. Singh AP and Singh HC (1984), Occupational Stress, Security—Insecurity and Job Involvement of First Level Industrial Supervisors, *Indian Journal of Industrial Relations*, Vol. 20, No. 2, Oct. 1984, pp. 174-185.

44. Holt, P., (1985): A Study of the Interaction of Levels of Occupational Stress, Degree of Burnout and Personality Hardiness in Female Elementary Teachers. *Unpublished Ph.D. Thesis*, University of Kansas.

45. Daniel C Ganster and Brunston T Mayes, Marcelline R Fusilier (1986), Role of Social Support in the Experience of Stress at Work, *Journal of Applied Psychology*, Vol. 71, No. 1, pp. 102-110.

46. Pestonjee DM (1987), Executive Stress: Should It Be Avoided? *Vikalpa*, 1987, 12, pp. 23-29.

47. Whitehead, J.T. (1987): Probation Officer Job Burnout: A Test of Two Theories, *Journal of Criminal Justice*, Vol. 15, 1-16.

48. Chatterjee A (1992), Commitment Cognitive Appraisal and Occupational Stress, *Productivity* [33(3), 393-400].

49. Singh AK and Sehgal P (1995), Men and Women in Transition Pattern of Stress Strain and Social Relations, *Vikalpa* [20(1), 13-22].

50. Mohammad Jamal, Job Stress, Satisfaction and Mental Health: An Empirical Examination of Self-Employed and Non Self-Employed Canadians, *Journal of Small Business Management.*

51. Hans Bosma, Richard Peter, Johannes Siegrist and Michael Marmot, Two Alternative Job Stress Models and the Risk of Coronary Heart Disease, *American Journal of Public Health*, January 1998, Vol. 88, No. 1.

52. Ashok K Sahni, Stress in Managers and Professionals in Indian Organizations, *Personnel Journal*, pp. 15-18.

53. Pandey CS (1998), A Study of Relationship Between Personality Dimensions and Organisational Role Stress in a Public Sector Organisation, *Indian Journal of Industrial Relations* [33(4), 506-516].

54. Luolu, (1999), Work Motivation, Job Stress and Employees' Well Being, *Journal of Applied Management Studies*, Vol. 8, No. 1, 1999.

55. Mishra PK and Rani DL (2001), Occupational Stress Among Working Women in Emerging Services, *Management and Labour Studies* [26(1), 25-36].

56. Cleopatra A Veloutsou and George G Panigyrahisb, Consumer Brand Managers' Job Stress, Job Satisfaction, Perceived Performance and Intention Leave, *Journal of Marketing Management*, 2004.

57. Andrew Marantz (2006), U. Mississippi: Editorial: Stress Management More Important Than Ever.

58. Sen (1987) Personal and Organisational Correlates to Role Stress and Coping Strategies Among Bank Employees, *The Journal of Education Administration*, [26(2), pp. 18-24]

59. Saranya A S (1999), Job Stress of Bank Employees, *Ph.D. Thesis.*

60. Howard, J.H., Rechnitzer P.A., and Cunningham D.A., (1975), Coping with Job Tensions—Effective and Ineffective Methods, *Public Personnel Management*, 4, pp. 317-326.

61. James C Quick and Janathan D Quick (1979), Reducing Stress Through Preventive Management, Personnel: Human Resource Management, *Fall*, 1979, pp 15-22.

62. Singh (1982), Psychological Correlates of Role Stress and Coping Styles for Working Women, *Human Relations*, 37, pp. 1036-1043.

63. Gupta and Murthy (1984), *Role Conflict and Coping Strategies—A Study on Indian Women (Unpublished Paper)*, Bangalore University, Bangalore.

64. Caplan, Naidu and Tripathi (1984), Coping and Defence: Constellations v/s. Components, *Journal of Health and Social Behaviour*, [25, pp.303-320].

65. Singh and Sinha (1985), Relationship of Coping Strategies with Job Related Strain, *Advances in Psychology* [1, pp 8-15].

66. Tandon (1986), Development of a Measure of Stress Tolerance, *Unpublished Doctoral Thesis*, University of Allahabad, Allahabad.

67. Susan McCammon et al (1987), Managing Workplace Stress, *Processes*, 40, pp. 346-368.

68. Gupta (1989), Role Stress, Locus of Control, Coping Styles and Role Efficacy: A Study of First Generation Entrepreneurs, *M.Phil Dissertation*, Delhi University, Delhi.

69. Mehta (1989), Appraisal of Stress and Coping in College Students, *M.Phil Dissertation*, Bangalore University, Bangalore.

70. Maureen H. Schnittger, Gloria W Bird (1990), Coping Among Dual-Career Men and Women Across the Family Life Cycle, *Psychological Reports*, January, 68 (3), pp. 958-962.

71. Singh (1990), Coping Strategies as Moderator of the Relationship Between Organisational Role Stress and Mental Health, *Ph.D. Thesis*.

72. Gary F Koeske, Stuart A Kirk, Randi D Koeske (1993), Coping with Job Stress: which Strategies Work Best?, *Journal of Occupational and Organisational Psychology*, 66, 319-335.

73. Ray, Eileen Berlin and Miller, Katherine I (1994), Social Support: Home/Work Stress and Burnout, Who Can Help?, *Journal of Applied Behavioural Science*, Vol. 30, Issue 3, p. 357.

74. Ahmed, Bhatt and Ahmad (1990), Stress and Coping Strategies Among Executive Technocrats. *Unpublished Paper Referred in D.M. Pestonjee, Stress and Coping*, New Delhi, Sage, 1992.

75. Sanders D (1999), Post Office Counters Stress, IRS Employment Review, No. 693, Dec. 1999, *Employee Health Bulletin* 12, pp 8-11.

76. Tansik D.A. and Routhieaux R (1999), Customer Stress-relaxation: The Impact of Music in a Hospital Waiting Room, *International Journal of Service Industries Management*, Vol. 10, No. 1, 1999, pp. 68-81.

77. Luthar H.K. (1999), Learning the Tao of Meditation Training, Workforce, Feb. 1999, *Real HR Real Impact, Supplementary*, pp. 10-11.

78. Briner R (2000), Stress Management: Effectiveness of Interventions, IRS Employment Review, No. 717, Dec. 2000, *Employee Health Bulletin* 18, pp. 12-17.

79. Atkinson (2000), When Stress Won't Go Away, *HR Magazine*, Vol. 45, No. 12, Dec. 2000, pp. 104-110.

80. Cristallini V (2000), Stress and the Improvement of Working Conditions: An Individual and Collective Responsibility, *Gestion* 2000 Vol. 17, No. 5, Sep.-Oct, 2000, pp. 15-33.

81. Yandrick R.M. (2000), Getting by with a Little Help from Friends, *HR Magazine*, Vol. 45, No. 10, Oct. 2000, pp. 102-104, 106, 108-109.

82. Hill C (2000), Counselling: A Primary Stress Intervention, IRS Employment Review, No. 705, June 2000, *Employee Health Bulletin* 15, pp. 15-19.

83. Harrington T (2000), Managing the Pressure, *Channel Business*, Feb. 2000, pp. 28, 30, 32.

84. Wah L (2000), The Emotional Tightrope, *Management Review*, Vol. 89, No. 1, Jan. 2000, pp. 38-43.

85. Shailendra Singh and Arvind L Sinha, Empirical Dimensions of Strategies of Coping with Job Related Stress, *Indian Journal of Applied Psychology*, Vol. 24(1), pp. 25-29.

86. Wustemann L (2002), Emotional Intelligence and the Bottom Line: Stress in the Supermarket, *Competency Emotional Intelligence*, Vol. 9, No. 2, Winter 2001-02, pp. 28-30.

87. Anna West (2006), *Management: Stress: Coping Strategies for Employers*.

# Chapter–3

# ORGANISATIONAL STRATEGIES FOR STRESS MANAGEMENT

*"Mind is the most powerful thing in the world. One who has controlled his mind can control anything in the world"*

—*Swami Sivananda*

## INTRODUCTION

It is natural that every one expects reasonable returns for the work turned out. But when one does not get either the reward or even appreciation it is natural that one gets frustrated. A common sight in organisations is that persons occupy positions not necessarily in consonance with their competence but due to several different extraneous factors operating. Organisations also inadvertently place round pegs in square holes resulting in dissatisfaction. This may be due to its roots in the organisational goals and personnel policies pursued when one indulges in path analysis.

When a hurdle is faced in attempting to achieve a goal, frustration is the outcome. No behaviour can be rated goalless. It depends upon the need deprivation level enabling the individual to make efforts to satisfy that need. In this process the needs may be deferrable depending upon the time available.

In the routine attempts to achieve goals hurdles are quite common, some surmountable and some insurmountable. The insurmountable hurdle is the cause of frustration and disappointment. Depending upon the level of determination of the individual, one might make another attempt with doubled vigour and some may middle-drop and shift the goal to something else. Frustration then may be said to be the outcome of privation and deprivation or conflict in regard to goal directed behaviour.

Growing organisations have the problems of stress which also is a part of life due to urbanisation, pollution, unchecked prices, ever increasing wants, unmet needs; all culminate into stress the individuals experience. No one can escape experiencing stress but one can surely attempt to utilise stress in a more productive way, in reducing dysfunctional stress and dealing effectively with it. The other terms more or less conveying the same meaning of stress are strain, conflict and pressure. In psychological terms stress is used to denote its effect on the individual. Conflict though used interchangeably, denotes more incompatibility. Stress is also used to symbolise a stimulus. For a safer understanding the term stressor for stimulus that produces stress, which has an effective (emotional) part of experience of incongruence, the term symptoms for physiological, behavioural and conceptual responses or changes and the term coping for behaviour to deal with emotional component of the experience of incongruence. The best example (Uday Pareek Organisational Behaviour Process p.166) is that in a musical instrument to produce fine music adequate tension is needed.

Organisations like families have specific roles for each person and each role is identified with certain functions and obligations. The position the role secures in the hierarchy bestows some powers, privileges and perks and the course responsibilities. The relationship between the roles is determined functionally and structurally. The concept of role is the key to the integration of the individual within the organisation. Each individual has a unique personality and needs while the organisation has its own structures and goals.

### A Framework to Explain How Stress Occurs

In order to understand the process of stress occurring, Cummings and Cooper (1979) have produced a theoretical framework. An individual will attempt to keep his life in a steady state. When faced with the threat of disruption to this secure state, the individual will experience stress. When faced with stress, two outcomes are possible. Firstly an individual might adjust his behaviour to enable himself to cope. Secondly, an individual may fail to cope with the stress causing it to continue. In this situation, it is probable that the continued stress may have negative effects.

From this framework, it could be argued that individuals can be taught strategies to enable them to cope and manage their stress more effectively.

### The Job Demands—Job Control Model (Karasek, 1979)

This model has become highly influential and has provided the basis for many studies on job stress over the years. The model looks at how a lack of control at work can contribute to workplace stress. Karasek argues that an individual's personal belief in his control over a work situation is of great importance. This model suggests that job strain, a stress outcome linked with physical and mental health problems, will occur in jobs that are high in demands and low in controllability. Karasek identified such jobs as 'high strain' jobs.

The model was used in a study on nurses by Fox et al. (1993). Their results have suggested that perhaps work related strain in nurses could be reduced if they could have given more control over their delivery of patient care and other aspects of their work. It is argued that this control could help nurses to better manage the demands placed upon them and in turn is likely to reduce their stress.

### Stress Management Intervention

There are a number of options to consider when looking at the prevention of stress in the workplace, which according to Cooper (1996), based on Murphy (1988), can be termed as primary, secondary, and tertiary levels of prevention. Primary prevention is concerned with taking action to reduce stressors or sources of stress. Secondary prevention is concerned with the detection and management of stress related symptoms by implementing stress management training. Tertiary prevention is concerned with the recovery process of individuals suffering from stress through stress counselling.

To develop an effective organisational strategy for stress management, employers need to integrate these three approaches.

### Management Intervention and Outcomes

DeFrank & Cooper (1987), according to Palmer & Dryden (1996), developed an expansion of perspective in a scheme viewing levels of stress management interventions and outcomes. They identified three levels, focussing on: the individual, the individual-organisational interface, and the organisation.

Interventions are needed at all levels, from the individual to the organisation. Most strategies are aimed toward the individual, but what is needed is a strategy to reduce organisational stressors and the provision of stress counselling within an organisation.

### Changing the Sources of Workplace Stress

There has been considerable activity in the stress management and counselling level but the organisational level strategies are relatively less common. This is because, particularly at organisational level, people cannot develop a global strategy as one size does not fit all. (However, Elkin & Rosch (1990) summarise a useful model for organisational strategies to reduce stress)

Many of the strategies at this level are aimed at increasing employee participation and autonomy. It has been recognised, according to Arnold et al (1998), that social support, control/ job discretion or autonomy and coping behaviour perform an important role in moderating the stress response.

Indirectly, many strategies, which focus on changing the style of work organisation, are often instruments for culture change, moving the organisation towards a more 'employee empowered' culture (Arnold et al, 1998). This is because employee participation has a positive impact on productivity and quality control (Arnold et al, 1998).

To alleviate the negative consequences of stress more effort on the part of policy makers, practitioners, and organisational management envisaged. It is therefore, a few efforts are made to suggest some effective measures that can alleviate the stress of bank employees and leads to their better adjustment within the organisation. They can be detailed as follows:

**Stress Management Programme**

It is considered to be necessary to organise a Stress Management Programme that focuses on different categories of employees at all hierarchical level. Many situational observations of employee-employer interaction identified within the organisation can lead to stress at work.

These include:

- Relationships with co-workers;
- An unsupportive supervisor;
- Fear towards management;
- Lack of consultation and communication;
- Too much interference with employees private, social or family life;
- Too much or too little to do;
- Too much pressure, unrealistic deadlines;
- Work that is too difficult or not demanding enough;
- Lack of control over the way the work is done;
- Poor working conditions;
- Being in the wrong job;

- Feeling undervalued;
- Feeling job difficulty;
- Insecurity and the threat of unemployment task.

Stress Management training programmes with specific human resource development goals in consultation with Senior Management may be organised for the employees of the banks.

**Prerequisites**

A successful Stress Management training programme requires the involvement and support of top officials and the cooperation from employees. It depends upon a clear plan, ongoing evaluations of progress, and clear goals for measuring success.

## STRESS MANAGEMENT STRATEGIES

Some of the organisational strategies are:

- **Time Management**

One of the ways to minimise stress and to make constructive use of stress, is to manage one's time more effectively. Time is the most scare resource available to an executive. The supply of time is totally and absolutely fixed. It cannot be augmented. And time lost is lost for ever. It can not be regained, recovered or replaced by something else. It cannot be accumulated like money. Time is thus the most valuable resource the executive possesses. And yet it is, wasted in innumerable way. Hence, an effective time management may reduce the stress by reducing the waste of time.

- **Time Log**

The time log is a simple technique which proves useful in analysing the activities that an executive is involved in, during the day. An analysis of the time log will reveal ways of improving the time utilisation. Log can be used to assess time utlisation on specific activities and tasks.

- **The Important/Urgent Matrix**

While analysing time, it is not sufficient to know what an individual has been doing each day. A deeper analysis of activities performed will also highlight how much time was spent on important and crucial tasks and how much on trivial and unimportant tasks. This matrix can help executives to analyse time they spend on different type of activities.

➤ **Diary for Time Planning**

Developing the own way to keep in the important information for ready access will be helpful what sort of information is needed to refer on a regular basis.

- Adequate steps are taken to redesign jobs, which are taxing to employees' abilities and capacities.
- The workload is reduced; role slimming and role adjustment process should be resorted to.
- The cross-functional and interdepartmental work arrangements are encouraged to reduce work related stress among low performers and low achievers.
- Role enlargement, role linkage and role enrichment to manage role isolation, self-role distance and role erosion are facilitated.
- Adequate role clarification is made whenever necessary to eliminate role ambiguity.
- More job oriented training programmes are introduced, which improve employees' skill and their confidence to work effectively.
- Career planning to manage role stagnation is concentrated.
- Open channel of communication to deal work related stress is encouraged.
- The employee is let to clear about hard work related reward and smart work related reward.
- Adequate resources i.e., material, technical and human, are extended to make employee feel safe and secure to perform their work effectively.
- Stress audit at all levels in the organisation is undertaken to identify stress area improving conditions of job and alleviating job stress.

- Justified use of grievance handling procedures is ensured to win trust and confidence of employees and reduce their anxiety and tension related to job related problems.
- Involvement of leaders and personnel at various levels in all phases of strategic interventions is encouraged to ensure successful and long-standing interventions.
- HRD interventions and individual stress alleviation programme are formulated.
- 'Pranayam' (Brain Stilling and control of Vital Force) as a holistic managerial strategy is introduced to deal with occupational strategy.
- Counselling on work related and personnel problems and support from a team of welfare health and counselling staff is provided.
- Attractive system of reward and recognition of good work are helpful in improving working environment for the employees.
- An organisational climate with career planning and career growth is useful to ensure further the retention of talented employees.
- The counselling practices are extended at employee family level including dependents and relatives.
- Effective follow up is made to different leave category absentee employees.
- Organiasations organise regular check up and those found suffering from very high stress should be subjected to stress management process.
- Excessive hours which directly affect the employee's physical fitness are cut back.
- Realistic self-concept among employees is developed such that it is neither inflated nor deflated.
- Management is encouraged to practice proactive approaches rather than reactive approaches as a strategic step.

## Industrial Stress Management

There are so many ISM's in the society today. And, many of them create in individuals a negative state of mind without being realised. However, they can learn techniques to overcome the negative side effects of those ISM's and learn to reverse them.

In everyday experiences, some of those ISM's have created in individuals a need to control, or, they find themselves in the position of being controlled by someone or something: at home, work, with children-even driving a car. Both controlling and being controlled can create a closed, negative state of mind. People need to relinquish control, and avoid being controlled.

Sometimes individuals become so overwhelmed by the daily negative pressures of ISM's that they affect their well-being. Depression, anxiety, disease, and disease enter their lives, originating, in part, from stress, emotional trauma, sadness, unforgiveness and other negative conditions.

Industrial Stress Management provides the means to work through and overcome adversity, stress and other negative cycles in the lives of individuals.

This programme could possibly help facilitate the employer company in minimizing employee's leaving due to job related stress, and anxiety, and could start to minimize high employee turnover. Industrial Stress Management techniques could begin to improve employer/employee relationships, and employee/ customer relationships at some level. In time, this could affect the bottom line in all ways.

## Coping Strategies and Positive Attitudes

THREE ATTITUDES TO APPROACH STRESS MANAGEMENT

### 1. *Accept*

One has to accept stress as part of life and build up resistance to its effects. Priorities should be set instead of focussing on the problem itself. "Learn to live with it" attitude should be adopted.

2. *Alter*

Situation is to be modified by understanding choices that are available. The choices are to change the situation, or to change any person.

3. *Avoid*

Unnecessary stressors should be avoided by recognising signs of stress and realising what provoked it.

**Individual Strategies for Stress Relief**

1. Humour in the situation is to be looked for as laughter is the best medicine.
2. One has to learn to forgive not only others but himself.
3. Some goals in life should be set and it is to be ensured that they are realistic.
4. Negative should be minimised and the positive should be maximised.
5. Exercise should be given to mind and body.
6. Limitations should be known, but abilities are to be focussed.
7. Relaxation techniques like deep breathing, progressive muscle relaxation, imagery, music may be practiced.
8. Each day should be begun with some deep breathing before one get out of bed. Mindful of the present moment, Clear the clutter of the rational mind and stop dwelling on the past and worrying about the future.
9. Physical, emotional, mental, and spiritual energy for things one can control should be used. While not all things are within the control, individuals can control a full range of their emotions. It should be remembered to get regular check ups from their physician, take care of health on all levels and have a support person to assist them in coping with their stress.
10. Attention should be availed to what one affirms. There are 60,000 thoughts a day. 95 per cent of the time, one has

those same 60,000 thoughts the next day. Individuals want those thoughts to be positive filled with positive affirmations of themselves. Inner chatter be allowed to inner champion rather than.

11. Take control by taking action. True priorities should be given by making lists and being in alignment with what matters most to honour. People have longings but they often don't achieve them because they make excuses. Start now and complete one action step at a time toward achieving the goal.
12. Financial health should be taken care of. This is a huge stress for many but it doesn't have to be. Begin with balancing the cheque book, make a list of expenses and learn to cut expenses or increase income. Financial Planner should be controlled in it is not having difficulty and not afford to.
13. Gossip, negativity and criticism should be left as it is. These are toxic behaviours. What matters most are and not what others have to say about one should be ignored. One has to be a balcony person for himself and others. He should be up in the balcony cheering for him and others.
14. Humour and laughter may be used daily. This is one of the top coping strategies for stress reduction. As adults get so serious and forget to laugh. Remind them of something funny and laugh many times each day. It loosens up the abdomen and relaxes the solar plexus. Watching comedy and reading the funnies and makes time for joy!
15. Let go of trying to be perfect. Perfection doesn't exist. Learn to cut corners and not be perfect. It takes far too much energy trying to be perfect. One has to learn to let go and relax.
16. Muscles of the Soul are to be exercised. Just as physical muscles will atrophy if it is not, the same will occur with muscles of the soul. What are muscles of the soul? Faith, hope, courage, humour, optimism, love, joy, balance will enable a person to cope up with stress.

17. One has to be open to change. Humans are resistant to change. In fact, the only human that seems to welcome change is a wet baby! Individuals have to learn to accept change as something positive in their life. Change is good in many ways. By opening up to receive change an individual opens himself up to new beginnings and limitless possibilities.

Learning assertive coping strategies for dealing with stress is an important mental health skill. Unfortunately, this skill is seldom modelled. The media often portray aggressive reactions as glamorous and desirable ways to deal with strong feelings, especially anger.

Assertive reactions reduce stress by allowing people to take steps to resolve the feelings. Passive and aggressive reactions may provide an immediate outlet, but usually create additional stress over time.

Whenever an individual is facing a situation or a problem that is causing distress, a critical analysis of the problem may help him plan out a strategy that may resolve the problem and ease out stress. If resolving the problem is beyond his control, then it is very important to manage the stress levels so as to prevent any physiological and psychological problems. A combination of physical and mental relaxation techniques will be of extreme help.

Physical and mental activities help manage stress. Physical activity is an especially good coping strategy, because it uses the bodily changes that are produced in the fight or flight response. People can determine the coping strategies that work best for them.

The physical and mental strategies are furnished hereunder:

**Physical Strategies**

- Any physical activity
- Jogging

- Dancing
- Swimming
- Gymnastics
- Relaxation techniques
- Massage

**Mental Strategies**

- Crossword puzzles
- Watching TV
- Having a hobby
- Talking to a friend
- Going to a movie
- Playing a game
- Listening to music
- Writing in a journal

**Environmental Strategies**

Stress and anxiety can prematurely age the mind and body of an individual. If not dealt with effectively, chronic stress and worrying can place undue strain upon the cardiovascular and immune systems. It can also make people prone to mood disorders and negatively affect their cognitive functions. Having a safe and comfortable place where individuals can relax and unwind can help improve their well-being and produce feelings of peace and tranquility.

Ideally, creating an atmosphere that induces calmness throughout the home is best coping strategy. However, if space is limited, individuals still can create their own oasis, even if it is in only a corner of a room or in a cubical at work. Here are eight easy ways to make personal space a true comfort zone.

**Tranquil Sounds**

Favourite music, sound machines and water falls can help individuals relax and unwind. Sounds have the ability to alter the perceptions and instantly change their moods.

### Living Plants

Live plants create a peaceful atmosphere. They improve the ambiance and air quality of indoor environments, and induce a positive energy around them.

### Soft Lighting

Soft and adjustable lighting can create a soothing atmosphere. Look for light bulbs that are bright, but not harsh. Being able to adjust the brightness of lighting will give people more control of the mood of their space.

### Pleasant Smells

A fresh and pleasant odour can transport people to a peaceful place and time. Open a window to get an exchange of air, use air purifiers or deodorizers to create the scent them find most pleasing.

### Furniture Arrangement

Furniture and other items should be placed to best fit the daily needs and actions. Personalising space with things that bestow happy memories will eliminate stress.

### Comfortable Textures

Pillows, throws and soft materials may be used to create a comfort zone. The sense of touch has a powerful impact upon feelings.

### Symbols of Nature

Bringing the outdoors inside with shells, rocks, feathers, wood, leaves, etc. may please the employees.

### Answering Machine

When one needs to unwind and revitalise, he has to turn his answering machine on and the volume down. One can always return calls when he is recharged and ready to talk.

Take control of surroundings, whether they are just a corner of a room or a desk at work. People can even use these steps when travelling to help them unwind. By creating their own personal oasis, they will be better able to relax and rejuvenate. A few changes may be all that they need to make themselves calm, peaceful, energised and inspired.

## CONCLUSION

People routinely encounter lots of distressing situations in their professional life. Organisational strategies are aimed at reducing job stress. Stress can be easily avoided or managed through proper management techniques like time management, workflow management etc. If the critical analysis of the problem suggests incorporation of a management technique, it is always advisable to implement such strategies in order to ease out the stressful situation and also avoid such situations in future.

# Chapter–4

# ANALYSIS AND INTERPRETATION

## INTRODUCTION

Stress has become a major concern of the modern times as it can cause harm to employees' health and performance. As living human makes constant demands, so it produces pressure, i.e., stress. Stress is, therefore, a natural and unavoidable feature of human life. However, stress beyond a particular level can cause psychological and physiological problems which in turn would affect the individual's performance in the organisation. Thus, the management of stress has become a challenging job for the modern organisations.

In the present chapter, the analysis and interpretation of the study "Occupational Stress and Coping Strategies" conducted on the employees of public sector and private sector banks in Erode District, Tamil Nadu are presented. The data collected were redrafted and tabulated in order to analyse the causes and effects of occupational stress and the coping strategies followed by the bank employees.

The following statistical tools were also applied to fulfil the objectives of the study.

- Chi-square Analysis

- Factor Analysis
- Discriminant Analysis
- Correlation Analysis
- Weighted Average
- Analysis of Varianace (ANOVA)

***Chi-Square Analysis***

Chi-square is a measure which evaluates the extent to which a set of the observed frequencies of a sample deviates from the corresponding set of the theoretical frequencies of the sample. It is a measure of the aggregate discrepancy between the actual frequencies and the theoretical frequencies in a sample. Chi-square is used as a test statistic in testing a hypothesis that provides a set of theoretical frequencies with which observed frequencies are compared.

The measure of chi-square enables to find out the degree of discrepancy between observed frequencies and theoretical frequencies and thus to determine whether the discrepancy so obtained is due to error of sample or due to chance. In this study it is used to test the significance of the relationship of demographic and job related variables with level of job stress.

**Factor Analysis**

Factor analysis is a multivariate technique. It is an extremely powerful and useful analytic approach to psychological, behavioural, financial and other types of data. It is a statistical technique for determining the underlying factors or forces among a large number of interdependent variables or measures. It is a method for extracting common factor potentially conveying a great deal of information. It tells what variables belong together – which ones virtually measure the same thing. It is an appropriate technique for cases where the variables have a high degree of intercorrelation. A factor is a construct, a hypcthetical entity that is assumed to underlie tests, scales, items or any other measures. In the present study, factor analysis has been employed to identify the sources of job stress and examine the significant stress coping strategies.

**Discriminant Analysis**

Discriminant analysis is a statistical technique which allows to study the differences between two or more groups with respect to several variables simultaneously and provide a means of classifying any object/individual into the group with which it is most closely associated and to infer the relative importance of each variable used to discriminate between different groups. A linear combination of predictor variables weighted in such a way that it will best discriminate among groups with the least error is called a linear discriminant function.

A discriminant function is a regression equation with a dependent variable that represents group membership. This function maximally discriminates the members of the group; it tells to which group each member probably belongs. It can be used to assign individuals to groups on the basis of their scores on two or more measures. From those scores, the 'best' composite score based on least-squares is calculated. Then the higher $R^2$ is the better predictor of the group membership.

For the purpose of the analysis, in this study employees have been classified into two groups such as high and low stress groups based on the level of stress. Discriminant function analysis has been used to identify the stressors which discriminate between the high and low stress groups.

**Correlation Analysis**

Correlation is a statistical technique which measures and analyses the degree or extent to which two or more variables fluctuate with reference to one another. Correlation thus denotes the inter-dependence amongst variables. The degrees are expressed by a coefficient which ranges, between -1 and +1. The direction of change is indicated by + or-signs; the former, refers to the sympathetic movement in the same direction and the latter, in opposite directions.

In this study, it is used to understand the relationship between personality type and the stress management ability of bank employees.

### Weighted Average Analysis

Weighted average analysis is applied for multi-response variables. In case several factors contribute to a particular aspect, weighted average analysis is the best suitable measurement for analysing the multi-responses. For each such response, weighted score will be assigned.

The ranks will then be awarded to the responses based on the weighted score. In the present study, weighted average analysis has been used to determine the order of individual and organisational effects caused by the stressors and to identify the most effective coping strategies adopted by bank employees.

### Analysis of Variance (Anova)

It is a statistical technique of testing whether the means of a specified classification differ significantly. Analysis of variance has been used to study the relationship between demographic and job related variables and level of adoption of stress coping strategies and also to study whether the stressors differ according to differences in the demographic variables and job related variables.

The analysis of data has been done after conducting the reliability test. The reliability index ascertained by the Alpha co-efficient method for the questionnaire as a whole is 0.7910.

## OBJECTIVES 1 AND 2

The first two objectives are: to measure the level of occupational stress of bank employees and to examine the factors influencing level of job stress. In this part of the study, an attempt has been made to fulfil these objectives. Chi-square test has been used to identify the variables influencing the level of occupational stress of bank employees.

### *Level of Occupational Stress and Influencing Factors*

Employees' level of stress has been determined on a five point scale on the Likert Model as explained in page 13 of Chapter 1. Based on the scores, stress level has been classified into three such as high (scores above 94) medium (scores between 62 and 94) and low (scores below 62).

Table 4.1 shows this classification. All the tables in this chapter have been compiled from the survey data.

**Table 4.1**

**Level of Job Stress**

| *Stress Level* | *No. of Respondents* | *Percentage* |
|---|---|---|
| Low | 65 | 16 |
| Medium | 252 | 63 |
| High | 83 | 21 |
| **Total** | **400** | **100** |

As per Table 4.1, higher percentage of the bank employees' (63) level of job stress is medium followed by 21 per cent with high stress and 16 per cent with low level of job stress. Factors influencing the level of job stress were analysed as follows:

**Age and Level of Job Stress**

Age is considered as a crucial factor in determining the attitudes and behaviour of human beings. Job stress may differ from one person to another depending upon their perception towards job. Perception is the view in which one understands a concept. Whether the job is stressful, and if so, to what extent is dependent on the perception of the employees towards their job. In this part of the analysis, an attempt has been made to study the level of job stress of different age groups of the sampled bank employees.

For this purpose, age of the employees has been classified as below 35 years, 35-50 years and above 50 years. The level of job stress has been divided into low, medium and high based on the job stress scores.

The mean stress scores are given in Table 4.2.

Table 4.2

Age and Job Stress – Mean Scores

| *S. No.* | *Age* | *No. of respondents* | *%* | *Mean Score* | *Range* | | *S.D.* |
|---|---|---|---|---|---|---|---|
| | | | | | *Min* | *Max* | |
| 1. | Below 35 years | 76 | 19.0 | 110.2 | 77 | 145 | 19.4 |
| 2. | 36-50 years | 215 | 53.8 | 104.6 | 56 | 150 | 17.5 |
| 3. | Above 50 years | 109 | 27.2 | 99.1 | 67 | 147 | 17.2 |
| | **Total** | **400** | **100** | | | | |

From Table 4.2 it is evident that the mean job stress score was the highest (110.2) among the respondents belonging to the age group of below 35 years and the lowest (99.1) among those above 50 years old. So there is inverse relationship between age and level of stress.

Table 4.3 shows the level of job stress of respondents of different age groups computed on the basis of the stress scores.

Table 4.3

Age and Level of Job Stress (Two-way Table)

| *S. No.* | *Age* | *Level of Job Stress* | | | *Total* |
|---|---|---|---|---|---|
| | | *Low* | *Medium* | *High* | |
| 1. | Below 35 years | 8<br>(10.5) | 44<br>(57.9) | 24<br>(31.6) | 76<br>(100) |
| 2. | 36-50 years | 30<br>(14.0) | 134<br>(62.3) | 51<br>(23.7) | 215<br>(100) |
| 3. | Above 50 years | 27<br>(24.8) | 74<br>(67.9) | 8<br>(7.3) | 109<br>(100) |
| | **Total** | **65** | **252** | **83** | **400** |

According to Table 4.3, the level of job stress is medium for majority of all the age groups. In respect of old age group (i.e. above 50 years), high level of job stress was found among low percentage of the respondents (7.3 per cent). Among those with high level of job stress, higher percentage (31.6) belongs to those below 35 years.

The following null hypothesis has been framed to test the significance of relationship between age and level of job stress.

*Null Hypothesis:* There is no significant difference among employees belonging to different age groups as regards level of job stress.

**Table 4.4**

**Age and Level of Job Stress (Chi-square Test)**

| *Factor* | *Calculated Value* | *Table Value* | *D.F.* | *Significance* |
|---|---|---|---|---|
| **Age** | 22.500 | 9.488 | 4 | Significant at 5% level |

### Inference

The null hypothesis is rejected as the calculated $\chi^2$ value exceeds the table value. It is concluded that lower the age, higher is the job stress.

### Gender and Level of Job Stress

There is physiological and natural difference between men and women. Something more is also created by society and that difference changes according to place and time. It is called 'gender disparity', a phenomenon different from 'sex difference'. The 'gender disparity' may make the job stressful. In order to analyse whether 'gender difference' causes the stress, the stress scores of the gender groups were calculated. Table 4.5 presents this information.

**Table 4.5**

**Gender and Job Stress – Mean Scores**

| *S. No.* | *Gender* | *No. of Respondents* | *%* | *Mean Score* | *Range* | | *S.D.* |
|---|---|---|---|---|---|---|---|
| | | | | | *Min* | *Max* | |
| 1. | Male | 337 | 84.3 | 103.4 | 56 | 150 | 17.9 |
| 2. | Female | 63 | 15.7 | 108.1 | 76 | 144 | 19.1 |
| | **Total** | **400** | **100** | | | | |

Table 4.5 denotes that mean stress score has been higher (108.1) for female employees when compared to the male employees (103.4).

Further, stress levels were ascertained. Table 4.6 shows the levels of job stress of the male and female respondents.

**Table 4.6**

**Gender and Level of Job Stress (Two-Way Table)**

| *S. No.* | *Gender* | *Level of Job Stress* | | | *Total* |
|---|---|---|---|---|---|
| | | *Low* | *Medium* | *High* | |
| 1. | Male | 47<br>(13.9) | 222<br>(65.9) | 68<br>(20.2) | 337<br>(100) |
| 2. | Female | 18<br>(28.6) | 30<br>(47.6) | 15<br>(23.8) | 63<br>(100) |
| | **Total** | **65** | **252** | **83** | **400** |

From Table 4.6 it is found that, majority of both the male and female had medium level of job stress. High level of job stress was found among higher percentage of the female employees (23.8 per cent) when compared to the male category (20.2 per cent).

The significance of the relationship between gender and the level of job stress has been analysed.

*Null Hypothesis:* There is no significant difference between employees belonging to the two gender groups with respect to level of job stress.

**Table 4.7**

**Gender and Level of Job Stress (Chi-square Test)**

| *Factor* | *Calculated Value* | *Table Value* | *D.F.* | *Significance* |
|---|---|---|---|---|
| **Gender** | 9.760 | 5.991 | 2 | Significant at 5% level |

**Inference**

The calculated value of chi-square is greater than the table value at 5 per cent of level of significance for 2 degrees of freedom. Hence, the null hypothesis does not hold good. It means that there is a significant relationship between gender and the level of job stress.

From the above, it is concluded that the female employees are more prone to job stress than the male.

**Marital Status and Level of Job Stress**

In Indian society, marriage makes a lot of changes in one's life. It gives responsibility to both the men and women. It makes the people pleasant and sometimes it is harmful. Marriage plays a vital role in the life of every human being by giving better status than the bachelorhood. Hence, in this study, the level of job stress among bank employees has been studied with reference to their marital status.

Table 4.8 shows the distribution of respondents according to marital status and the job stress scores.

**Table 4.8**

**Marital Status and Job Stress – Mean Scores**

| *S. No.* | *Marital Status* | *No. of Respondents* | *%* | *Mean Score* | *Range* | | *S.D.* |
|---|---|---|---|---|---|---|---|
| | | | | | *Min* | *Max* | |
| 1. | Married | 369 | 92.3 | 103.2 | 56 | 150 | 17.5 |
| 2. | Unmarried | 31 | 7.7 | 115.6 | 78 | 144 | 21.0 |
| | **Total** | **400** | **100** | | | | |

Mean job stress score has been found to be higher (115.6) for the unmarried category than the married (103.2) implying high stress for the unmarried.

Level of job stress based on the stress scores is given in Table 4.9.

Table 4.9

**Marital Status and Level of Job Stress (Two-Way Table)**

| *S. No.* | *Marital Status* | *Level of Job Stress* | | | *Total* |
|---|---|---|---|---|---|
| | | *Low* | *Medium* | *High* | |
| 1. | Married | 63 (17.1) | 238 (64.5) | 68 (18.4) | 369 (100) |
| 2. | Unmarried | 2 (6.5) | 14 (45.2) | 15 (48.3) | 31 (100) |
| | **Total** | **65** | **252** | **83** | **400** |

It is found from Table 4.9 that majority of the married employees (64.5 per cent) were having medium level of job stress. On the other hand, most of the unmarried employees (48.3 per cent) were working with high level of job stress.

In order to study the significance of relationship between marital status and the level of job stress, the null hypothesis tested is, Employees' level of stress is independent of their marital status.

Table 4.10

**Marital Status and Level of Job Stress (Chi-Square Test)**

| *Factor* | *Calculated Value* | *Table Value* | *D.F.* | *Significance* |
|---|---|---|---|---|
| Marital Status | 16.053 | 5.991 | 2 | Significant at 5% level |

**Inference**

The null hypothesis is not true since the calculated $\chi^2$ value is greater than the table value.

Hence, it is concluded that marital status of employees causes differences in the level of job stress.

**Educational Qualification and Level of Job Stress**

Education gives knowledge to the people. Generally, the educated are prudent in taking critical decisions. Education leads to proper understanding of any situation. It develops patience among the human beings. Here, an attempt has been made to analyse the significance of the relationship between educational qualification and level of job stress. The educational qualification of bank employees has been classified as school level, graduate level and post graduate level.

Table 4.11 shows the mean stress scores of the three educational groups of respondents with range and standard deviation.

**Table 4.11**

**Educational Qualification and Job Stress – Mean Scores**

| *S. No.* | *Educational Qualification* | *No. of Respondents* | *%* | *Mean Score* | *Range* | | *S.D.* |
|---|---|---|---|---|---|---|---|
| | | | | | *Min* | *Max* | |
| 1. | School level | 26 | 6.5 | 97.9 | 67 | 145 | 18.2 |
| 2. | Graduate | 221 | 55.3 | 102.8 | 61 | 147 | 17.6 |
| 3. | Post Graduate | 153 | 38.2 | 107.2 | 56 | 150 | 18.4 |
| | **Total** | **400** | **100** | | | | |

As per Table 4.11, stress scores were found to be increasing with increase in the level of education indicating that higher the education, greater is the level of job stress.

Table 4.12 depicts the different levels of job stress of the educational categories determined on the basis of stress scores.

**Table 4.12**

**Educational Qualification and Level of Job Stress (Two-Way Table)**

| *S. No.* | *Educational Qualification* | *Level of Job Stress* | | | *Total* |
|---|---|---|---|---|---|
| | | *Low* | *Medium* | *High* | |
| 1. | School level | 8<br>(30.8) | 16<br>(61.5) | 2<br>(7.7) | 26<br>(100) |
| 2. | Graduate | 33<br>(14.9) | 148<br>(67.0) | 40<br>(18.1) | 221<br>(100) |
| 3. | Post Graduate | 24<br>(15.7) | 88<br>(57.5) | 41<br>(26.8) | 153<br>(100) |
| | **Total** | **65** | **252** | **83** | **400** |

Table 4.12 also, reveals that higher percentage of the high stress employees (26.8) belong to the Post Graduate category while majority of the low stress group (30.9 per cent) belong to the school educated category.

The significance of the relationship between education and level of job stress has been analysed by formulating the following null hypothesis which has been statistically tested.

*Null Hypothesis:* Differences in the level of education do not cause difference in the level of job stress.

**Table 4.13**

**Educational Qualification and Level of Job Stress (Chi-Square Test)**

| *Factor* | *Calculated Value* | *Table Value* | *D.F.* | *Significance* |
|---|---|---|---|---|
| **Educational qualification** | 12.996 | 9.488 | 4 | Significant at 5% level |

**Inference**

Educational qualificaztion and level of job stress have significant relationship. The null hypothesis does not hold good.

**Total Emoluments Drawn and Level of Job Stress**

Salary earned increases the savings, buying capacity, etc. At the same time, higher the salary, greater will be the responsibilities. The salary earned also gives safety and security for the family and life. It increases the happiness of employees.

In order to determine the stress level of employees stress scores were ascertained. Table 4.14 indicates the stress scores with summary statistics.

**Table 4.14**

**Salary Drawn and Job Stress – Mean Scores**

| *S. No.* | *Monthly Salary* | *No. of Respondents* | *%* | *Mean Score* | *Range* | | *S.D.* |
|---|---|---|---|---|---|---|---|
| | | | | | *Min* | *Max* | |
| 1. | Below Rs.15000 | 135 | 33.8 | 104.1 | 56 | 145 | 16.3 |
| 2. | Rs. 15000- Rs.20000 | 112 | 28.0 | 106.1 | 67 | 147 | 16.3 |
| 3. | Above Rs. 20000 | 153 | 38.2 | 102.8 | 61 | 150 | 20.7 |
| | **Total** | **400** | **100** | | | | |

From Table 4.14, it is noted that stress scores of respondents were lower for those drawing higher salary.

Table 4.15 presents the various levels of job stress of respondents categorised according to their salary.

**Table 4.15**

**Salary Drawn and Level of Job Stress (Two-Way Table)**

| *S. No.* | *Monthly Salary* | *Level of Job Stress* | | | *Total* |
|---|---|---|---|---|---|
| | | *Low* | *Medium* | *High* | |
| 1. | Below Rs. 15000 | 14 (10.4) | 96 (71.1) | 25 (18.5) | 135 (100) |
| 2. | Rs. 15000 - Rs. 20000 | 14 (12.5) | 78 (69.6) | 20 (17.9) | 112 (100) |
| 3. | Above Rs. 20000 | 37 (24.2) | 78 (51.0) | 38 (24.8) | 153 (100) |
| | **Total** | **65** | **252** | **83** | **400** |

Table 4.15 signifies that in all the three categories, majority of the respondents had medium level of job stress. Among the high stress group higher percentage constitute the employees with more than Rs. 20,000 monthly salary.

In order to understand the relationship between salary earned and level of job stress of bank employees, the following null hypothesis is tested.

*Null Hypothesis:* There is no significant difference among employees belonging to different salary groups with respect to level of stress.

**Table 4.16**

**Salary and Level of Job Stress (Chi-square Test)**

| *Factor* | *Calculated Value* | *Table Value* | *D.F.* | *Significance* |
|---|---|---|---|---|
| **Monthly salary** | 17.476 | 9.488 | 4 | Significant at 5% level |

**Inference**

It is observed from Table 4.16 that the relationship between salary and level of job stress is significant. Hence the null hypothesis is rejected.

**Type of Bank and Level of Job Stress**

The banks may be classified as private sector banks and public sector banks. The rules and regulations of banks may differ from each other. The work environment of one bank may differ from that of another. The level of job stress is analysed with reference to the type of banks.

Table 4.17 presents the stress scores of employees according to the type of bank.

Table 4.17

Type of Bank and Job Stress – Mean Scores

| *S. No.* | *Type of Bank* | *No. of Respondents* | *%* | *Mean Score* | *Range* | | *S.D.* |
|---|---|---|---|---|---|---|---|
| | | | | | *Min* | *Max* | |
| 1. | Private sector | 106 | 26.5 | 75.86 | 30 | 124 | 18.1 |
| 2. | Public sector | 294 | 73.5 | 76.85 | 33 | 119 | 18.2 |
| | **Total** | **400** | **100** | | | | |

From Table 4.17 it is found that the average job stress score was marginally higher among public sector bank employees and lower among the private sector bank employees.

Further, stress levels were determined based on the stress scores for the two bank groups, which are given in Table 4.18.

**Table 4.18**

**Type of Bank and Level of Job Stress (Two-Way Table)**

| *S. No.* | *Type of Bank* | *Level of Job Stress* | | | *Total* |
|---|---|---|---|---|---|
| | | *Low* | *Medium* | *High* | |
| 1. | Private Sector | 25 (23.6) | 65 (61.3) | 16 (15.1) | 106 (100) |
| 2. | Public Sector | 40 (13.6) | 187 (63.6) | 67 (22.8) | 294 (100) |
| | **Total** | **65** | **252** | **83** | **400** |

Table 4.18 reveals that high level of job stress was experienced by lower percentage (15.1) of the employees of private sector banks when compared to public sector banks (22.8 per cent).

*Null hypothesis:* There is no significant difference between employees belonging to the two types of banks as regards level of job stress.

Table 4.19

Type of Bank and Level of Job Stress (Chi-square Test)

| *Factor* | *Calculated Value* | *Table Value* | *D.F.* | *Significance* |
|---|---|---|---|---|
| **Type of bank** | 0.216 | 5.991 | 2 | Not Significant |

**Inference**

The calculated value of chi-square is less than the table value. The null hypothesis is hence accepted and it is concluded that the relationship between type of bank and level of job stress is not significant.

**Nature of Job and Level of Job Stress**

The employees of banks are working in different cadres like Manager, Assistant Manager, Officer, Clerk, etc. The employees, based on their post have to assume different responsibilities. Lack of support from others may lead to job stress. Hence, it is necessary to find out whether nature of job is a stressor for bank employees.

**Table 4.20**

**Nature of Job and Job Stress – Mean Scores**

| *S. No.* | *Nature of job / Post held* | *No. of Respondents* | *%* | *Mean Score* | *Range* | | *S.D.* |
|---|---|---|---|---|---|---|---|
| | | | | | *Min* | *Max* | |
| 1. | Manager | 128 | 32.0 | 100.1 | 61 | 150 | 18.8 |
| 2. | Assistant Manager | 38 | 9.4 | 99.1 | 62 | 126 | 18.8 |
| 3. | Officer | 63 | 15.8 | 105.3 | 65 | 132 | 15.9 |
| 4. | Clerk | 171 | 42.8 | 108.7 | 56 | 147 | 18.1 |
| | **Total** | **400** | **100** | | | | |

It is observed from Table 4.20 that mean stress scores were greater for clerks than the other categories of employees. The lowest job stress score was found for assistant managers. Based on the stress scores, level of stress were determined which are indicated in Table 4.21.

**Table 4.21**

**Nature of Job and Level of Job Stress (Two-Way Table)**

| *S. No.* | *Nature of job / Post held* | *Level of Job Stress* | | | *Total* |
|---|---|---|---|---|---|
| | | *Low* | *Medium* | *High* | |
| 1. | Manager | 31 (24.2) | 73 (57.0) | 24 (18.8) | 128 (100) |
| 2. | Assistant Manager | 13 (34.2) | 18 (47.4) | 7 (18.4) | 38 (100) |
| 3. | Officer | 7 (11.1) | 45 (71.4) | 11 (17.5) | 63 (100) |
| 4. | Clerk | 14 (8.2) | 116 (67.8) | 41 (24.0) | 171 (100) |
| | **Total** | **65** | **252** | **83** | **400** |

Level of job stress was found to be medium for higher percentage of all the categories as per Table 4.21.

Among the high stress group, higher percentage (24) belongs to the clerical cadre.

To test the significance of the relationship between nature of job and job stress, the null hypothesis that "Level of job stress is independent of employees' nature of job" has been formulated and tested.

**Table 4.22**

**Nature of Job and Level of Job Stress (Chi-square Test)**

| *Factor* | *Calculated Value* | *Table Value* | *D.F.* | *Significance* |
|---|---|---|---|---|
| **Nature of job** | 25.47 | 12.59 | 6 | Significant at 5% level |

**Inference**

Differences in the nature of job cause differences in the level of job stress.

**Length of Service and Level of Job Stress**

The length of service gives experience. Experience helps employees in gaining more knowledge, understanding and patience. At the same time, length of service leads to more accountability.

Table 4.23 shows the distribution of respondents based on their length of service and the stress scores indicating mean, minimum, maximum and standard deviation.

As per Table 4.23, mean scores were going down as length of service increased. So, shorter the period of service, greater is the stress, lowest stress score is found in the case of those with more than 10 years of service.

Based on stress scores, level of stress of employees differing in services was computed.

Table 4.23

**Length of Service and Job Stress – Mean Scores**

| *S. No.* | *Length of Service* | *No. of Respondents* | *%* | *Mean Score* | *Range* | | *S.D.* |
|---|---|---|---|---|---|---|---|
| | | | | | *Min* | *Max* | |
| 1. | Below 5 years | 105 | 26.3 | 106.3 | 62 | 150 | 18.0 |
| 2. | 6-10 years | 177 | 44.2 | 103.3 | 56 | 145 | 18.7 |
| 3. | Above 10 years | 118 | 29.5 | 103.1 | 61 | 147 | 17.3 |
| | **Total** | **400** | **100** | | | | |

Table 4.24 depicts the levels of job stress of the respondents with different periods of service.

Table 4.24

**Length of Service and Level of Job Stress (Two-Way Table)**

| *S. No.* | *Length of Service* | *Level of Job Stress* | | | *Total* |
|---|---|---|---|---|---|
| | | *Low* | *Medium* | *High* | |
| 1. | Below 5 years | 9 (8.6) | 71 (67.6) | 25 (23.8) | 105 (100) |
| 2. | 6-10 years | 38 (21.4) | 104 (58.8) | 35 (19.8) | 177 (100) |
| 3. | Above 10 years | 18 (15.3) | 77 (65.2) | 23 (19.5) | 118 (100) |
| | **Total** | **65** | **252** | **83** | **400** |

Table 4.24 shows that higher percentage (23.8) of the high stress group are those with less than 5 years of service. The significance of the relationship is tested.

*Null hypothesis:* There is no significant difference among employees having different periods of service with respect to level of stress.

Table 4.25

Length of Service and Level of Job Stress (Chi-square Test)

| *Factor* | *Calculated Value* | *Table Value* | *D.F.* | *Significance* |
|---|---|---|---|---|
| **Length of Service** | 9.457 | 9.488 | 4 | NS |

NS— Not Significant

**Inference**

There is no significant relationship between length of service and level of job stress. Hence the null hypothesis is true.

## OBJECTIVES 3 AND 4

The third objective of the study is to understand the sources of stress of the sampled respondents and analyse the influencing factors.

The fourth objective of the study is to identify the stressors which discriminate between employees of high stress and low stress.

These objectives have been dealt with, in this part of the study.

### *Sources of Job Stress*

Before presenting the analysis related to job stress, sources of job stress are explained here. The factors causing stress are called stressors. Review of studies relating to job stress indicated that the common stressors acting on employees may generate from individuals, groups, organisations or extra-organisational sources. Individual, group and organisational stressors are work stressors, while extra-organisational stressors are non-work stressors.

Individual stressors depend to a large extent on one's personality traits and constraints of change. The nature of an individual determines his personality traits. Constraints of change are the result of changes in one's career and life.

Lack of group cohesiveness, absence of leadership support, poor relationship with colleagues, superiors and subordinates are the group stressors.

Role factors, job factors and physical factors constitute organisational stressors. Role factors refer to role ambiguity, role conflict, role overload, role stagnation and inadequacy of role authority. Job factors include difficulty in performing the job, feeling of inequity, feeling of being poorly paid and mismatch between one's capability and requirements of the job. Poor lighting, ventilation, noise levels, etc. constitute physical factors. Extra-organisational factors consist of family problems, financial difficulties, and conflict of family demands with organisational demands.

Thus sources of stress are many. The major sources of stress for the sampled bank employees have been analysed based on 30 statements measuring stressors on a five point scale on the Likert model ranging from Strongly Agree to Strongly Disagree.

*Factor Analysis*

The responses thus collected were analysed using 'Factor Analysis' technique, to identify the most significant factors causing job stress among bank employees. Factor analysis has been carried out by following Principal Component Analysis with Varimax rotation.

For interpretation of factors, factor loadings greater than 0.38 for a sample of 400 is considered to be significant (Harman, 1967). The factor structure of the population is explored and ten factors are extracted. These factors were used as variables for further analysis.

For interpretation of factors, greater weights were given to high loading variables. Keeping in view, the nature of the high loading variables, the factors are interpreted and named. The results of the factor analysis are presented as follows:

The first factor accounts for 11.69 per cent of the total variations. This factor has significant loadings on five statements. These statements measure Role Ambiguity and Role Authority. The factor loadings of these variables are shown in Table 4.26.

### Table 4.26

### Significant Loadings of Variables on Varimax Factor I

| *St. No.* | *Statements* | *Loadings* |
|---|---|---|
| B 10 | I get improper guidance | 0.677 |
| B 16 | I feel insignificant and powerless in the organisation | 0.666 |
| B 17 | My working hours are inconvenient | 0.613 |
| B 26 | I have no power to discipline my subordinates | 0.586 |
| B 21 | Changes in work environment due to technological upgradation is disturbing me | 0.555 |

All the statements are positively loaded as per Table 4.26. High positive loadings on statements 10 and 16 denote that job stress arises due to misunderstanding of the role to be played and lack of clarity of work. Statement 17 indicates that inconvenient working hours cause job stress. Statements 26 and 21 imply that the job stress is caused by lack of authority and extra factors. Since all the statements reflect the presence of unfavourable work climate which results in stress, the first factor is termed as *'Role Ambiguity and Absence of Role Authority'* (*Organisational – Role factor*).

The second factor consists of five variables. This factor extracted a variance of 10.21 per cent of the total variance. Most of these statements are aimed at measuring "Role overload". The significant loadings of variables under factor II are presented in Table 4.27.

### Table 4.27

### Significant Loadings of Variables on Varimax Factor II

| *St. No.* | *Statements* | *Loadings* |
|---|---|---|
| B 14 | I work under extreme time pressure | 0.774 |
| B 7 | I experience work pressure often | 0.699 |
| B 13 | I have to perform tasks that are too difficult | 0.640 |
| B 8 | I feel that the leadership in our organisation is inappropriate | 0.601 |
| B 9 | My superior's behaviour is inconsiderate | 0.576 |

The high positive loadings on "Statements 14, 7 and 13" indicate that job stress is caused by role overload. "Statement 8" shows that lack of leadership support causes job stress. Poor relationship with superiors is also a cause of job stress is emphasised by "Statement 9". Since all the statements reflect the presence of unfavourable work climate which arises due to excess work load, lack of leadership support and poor relationship with superiors, the second factor is termed as *"Role Overload and Lack of Leadership Support"(Organisational – Role factor)*.

The third factor extracted a variance of 8.78% of the total variance. The factor loadings on these variables are shown in Table 4.28.

**Table 4.28**

**Significant Loadings of Variables on Varimax Factor III**

| *St. No.* | *Statements* | *Loadings* |
|---|---|---|
| B 11 | There is no avenue for two way communication in our organisation | 0.749 |
| B 20 | There is no match between my abilities and the requirements of my job | 0.573 |
| B 15 | My opinion is not sought in solving organisational problems | 0.566 |
| B 12 | I often feel let down by superiors | 0.507 |
| B 22 | Job rotations have a negative influence on my job | 0.401 |

High positive loadings on "Statement 11" indicate how role stagnation affects the developmental attitude of the employees and thus causing stress in them. "Statements 20 and 15" show that there are positive loadings on these variables and there is a mismatch between the abilities of the employees and work assigned to them and due consideration was not given to them in solving the organisational problems. Job stress results when employees feel that their superiors let them down or rotations have a negative influence. Based on the above interpretation, the factor is named *"Role Stagnation and Mismatch" (Organisational – Role factor)*.

The significant loadings obtained on different statements of Factor IV are presented in Table 4.29. The fourth factor extracted a variance of 6.69 per cent of the total variance, and has high factor loadings on "Statements 5 and 23".

Table 4.29

**Significant Loadings of Variables on Varimax Factor IV**

| *St. No.* | *Statements* | *Loadings* |
|---|---|---|
| B 5 | I feel anxious and apprehensive when I am at work | 0.747 |
| B 23 | I feel that I am not learning enough in my present job for taking up higher responsibilities in future | 0.591 |

High positive loadings on 'Statements 5' denote that fear and concern about the job leads to job stress among bank employees. 'Statement 23' indicates that lesser opportunity for learning is a cause of job stress. Hence, this factor can be termed as *"Role anxiety and feeling of inequity"* (*Organisational – Job factor*).

The significant loadings obtained on different statements of Factor V are presented in Table 4.30. The fifth factor extracted a variance of 6.21 per cent of the total variations, and has got high factor loadings on "Statements 18 and 19"

Table 4.30

**Significant Loadings of Variables on Varimax Factor V**

| *St. No.* | *Statements* | *Loadings* |
|---|---|---|
| B 18 | I feel that my salary is less in comparison with the quantity of my labour | 0.763 |
| B 19 | Opportunities for learning and rise in my career are fewer | 0.430 |

Very high importance being accorded to salary and other opportunities show the strong link between 'stress' and 'monetary and non-monetary benefits'. Unsatisfactory pay and lack of other opportunities result in job dissatisfaction leading to job stress. Thus this factor is named as *"Feeling of being paid low"* (*Organisational – Job factor*).

The sixth factor contributed a variance of 6.47 per cent of the total variance. Table 4.31 presents the factor loading on the "Statements 30 and 27".

Table 4.31

Significant Loadings of Variables on Varimax Factor VI

| *St. No.* | *Statements* | *Loadings* |
|---|---|---|
| B 30 | The following non-work environment had a negative influence on my job:<br>(i) Family relocation<br>(ii) Financial problems<br>(iii) Illness of my family members | 0.725 |
| B 27 | Changes in my work environment due to transfers/promotions have disrupted the routine of my daily life | 0.677 |

Resistance to change is the nature of human beings. Thus any change in the job or work atmosphere creates hesitation among the human beings for being adapted to such change and thus may be one of the reasons causing job stress among bank employees.

Positive factor loadings on "Statements 30 and 27" indicate that change in the job due to transfers/promotions and personal problems like family relocation, financial problems and illness of family members create stress due to the challenge of facing a new work atmosphere and a new job and also physical strain. Therefore, this factor is named as *"Extra organisational factor"*.

The seventh factor accounted for 6.37 per cent of the total variations. "Statements 1 and 3" constituted the seventh factor. Table 4.32 presents the factor loadings on these statements.

Negative loadings on the "Statements 1 and 3" reveal that lack of support from colleagues and subordinates create stress among bank employees. Lack of cordial relationship with co-workers and non-cooperation from subordinates may create job stress. In the present analysis, the factor loadings on these statements are negative. Hence, these variables contribute to the job stress among bank employees. This factor is named as *"Lack of Interpersonal relationship"* (*Group factor*).

Table 4.32

Significant Loadings of Variables on Varimax Factor VII

| *St. No.* | *Statements* | *Loadings* |
|---|---|---|
| B 1 | I maintain cordial relationship with co-workers | - 0.784 |
| B 3 | My subordinates are very co-operative | - 0.660 |

The proportion of variance of the eighth factor on total variance stood at 5.27 per cent. This factor has been constituted by "Statements 25, 24 and 6". Table 4.33 shows the factor loadings on these statements.

Table 4.33

Significant Loadings of Variables on Varimax Factor VIII

| *St. No.* | *Statements* | *Loadings* |
|---|---|---|
| B 25 | I do not have the patience to answer customer queries | 0.780 |
| B 24 | I get irritated by the behaviour of customers | 0.608 |
| B 6 | The work assigned to me is monotonous | 0.430 |

High positive loadings on 'Statements 25, 24 and 6' reflect the personality trait of the individual employees. It indicates the serious nature of employees' feelings cause job stress. Responding to customer related queries and behaviour are influenced by the personality trait of the employees. 'Statement 6' indicates the lack of variety in the job. It may lead to dissatisfaction on the job and thus causes job stress. Keeping this interpretation in mind, Factor VIII may be termed as *"Personality Trait"*, which causes stress (*Individual factor*).

Table 4.34 presents significant factor loadings on variables for Factor IX. The ninth factor contributed a variance of 5.09 per cent to the total variations.

Table 4.34

Significant Loadings of Variables on Varimax Factor IX

| *St. No.* | *Statements* | *Loadings* |
|---|---|---|
| B 2 | My job assignments are easier | - 0.789 |
| B 4 | I am able to complete the work assigned to me | - 0.521 |

Negative loadings on 'Statement 2' indicate that there is difficulty in performing the job, which creates job stress. 'Statement 4' shows that the inability in performing the job and work pressure are sources of stress among bank employees. Hence, this factor has been termed as *"Difficulty in performing the job"* (*Job factor*).

The tenth and the last factor accounted for about 4.70 per cent of the total variations. Table 4.35 shows the factor loadings on these statements.

Table 4.35

Significant Loadings Variables on Varimax Factor X

| *St. No.* | *Statements* | *Loadings* |
|---|---|---|
| B 28 | Inter-group and Intra-group conflicts in the organisation disrupts me often | 0.794 |
| B 29 | My responsibilities are poorly defined which leads to clash of interests | 0.476 |

High positive loadings on the 'Statement 28' reveal that lack of unity among the members of inter-group and intra-group shatters the understanding among them. It denotes that there is a lack of group cohesiveness. Positive loadings on 'Statement 29' denote that improper role description leads to job stress. Hence, this factor is termed as *"Lack of group cohesiveness and Role description"* (*Group factor*).

Based on the significant stressors identified and broadly classified such as individual factors, group factors, organisational factors (comprising of role factors and job factors) and extra-organisational factors, further analysis has been made to understand whether stressors differ according to the difference in the demographic and job related variables, through Analysis of Variance (ANOVA). Relevant hypotheses were formulated in this connection.

Only summary tables of ANOVA 'F' ratios have been presented in the chapter.

The analysis is presented as follows:

***Stressors and Demographic Variables***

### Stressors and Age Groups

Here, an attempt has been made to study the relationship between sources of stress of bank employees and their age. In this context, Analysis of Variance is performed and the results have been presented in Table 4.36.

*Null Hypothesis:* There is no significant difference among employees belonging to the different age groups with respect to stressors.

**Table 4.36**

**Summary of ANOVA 'F' Ratios for Causes of Stress with Respect to Age**

| | *1* | *2* | *3* | | *4* |
|---|---|---|---|---|---|
| *Causes* | *Individual Factors* | *Group Factors* | *Organisational Factors* | | *Extra Organisational Factors* |
| | | | *Role Factors* | *Job Factors* | |
| F Ratios | 11.4024 * | 3.5168 * | 8.6589 * | 5.0317 * | 3.7325 * |

* Significant at 5% level.

Table 4.36 shows that the relationship between age and all types of stressors is significant. The value of 'F' has been found to be greater than the table value at 5 per cent level of significance. Hence, the null hypothesis has been rejected and it is concluded that stressors differ according to difference in age.

When comparing the age with stressors, individual factors have contributed more towards the stress than the other factors. The challenges of dealing with changes in job had been the most significant individual factor, which contributes most to the stress. This factor has been followed by role factors and job factors such as role overload and role anxiety. The non-work environment stress is caused by family relocation, financial problems and illness of the family members of the employees.

## Gender and Sources of Stress

With a view to analyse whether stressors differ significantly for the gender groups of bank employees, the following null hypothesis has been framed.

*Null Hypothesis:* There is no significant difference between employees belonging to the two gender groups with respect to stressors.

**Table 4.37**

**Summary of ANOVA 'F' Ratios for Causes of Stress with Respect to Gender**

| *Causes* | *1* | *2* | *3* | | *4* |
|---|---|---|---|---|---|
| | *Individual Factors* | *Group Factors* | *Organisational Factors* | | *Extra Organisational Factors* |
| | | | *Role Factors* | *Job Factors* | |
| **F Ratios** | 1.1563 (NS) | 0.1457 (NS) | 3.3951 (NS) | 2.9511 (NS) | 2.0712 (NS) |

NS— Not Significant

Table 4.37 shows no significant results for the stressors. The results show that individual stressors and gender are independent. Group factors have no significant relationship with the gender. It is understood that gender does not influence the role factors. The job factors do not have any significant relationship with the gender of the bank employees. Similarly, stress from extra organisational factors does not differ for male and female employees.

## Educational Qualification and Sources of Stress

In this part of the study, an attempt has been made to measure the relationship between educational qualification of the bank employees and sources of stress. The following null hypothesis has been framed to test the significance of relationship between education and sources of stress.

*Null Hypothesis:* There is no significant difference among employees belonging to the different educational levels with respect to stressors.

Table 4.38 shows the summary of ANOVA F ratios for sources of stress with respect to education.

**Table 4.38**

**Summary of ANOVA 'F' Ratios for Causes of Stress with Respect to Education**

| *Causes* | *1* | *2* | *3* | | *4* |
|---|---|---|---|---|---|
| | *Individual Factors* | *Group Factors* | *Organisational Factors* | | *Extra Organisational Factors* |
| | | | *Role Factors* | *Job Factors* | |
| **F Ratios** | 6.6367 * | 3.6212 * | 3.8371 * | 4.2258 * | 5.8127 * |

* Significant at 5% level.

Table 4.38 denotes that stressors differ for different educational levels. Individual factors of stress are the major stressors, which differ for the different educational levels of bank employees with a high F ratio. Extra organisational factors also make significant difference among the employees differing in their educational levels. There has been significant relationship between education of the bank employees and stress caused by role factors. Group factors account for the lowest variation in stress. Lack of patience to answer customer queries is the most significant individual factor which causes stress.

## Salary and Sources of Stress

Here, an attempt has been made to study the relationship between sources of stress of bank employees and their emoluments. In this context, Analysis of Variance is performed and the results have been presented in Table 4.39.

*Null Hypothesis:* There is no significant difference among employees belonging to the different levels of salary with respect to stressors.

Table 4.39

Summary of ANOVA 'F' Ratios for Causes of Stress with Respect to Salary

| | *1* | *2* | *3* | | *4* |
|---|---|---|---|---|---|
| *Causes* | *Individual Factors* | *Group Factors* | *Organisational Factors* | | *Extra Organisational Factors* |
| | | | *Role Factors* | *Job Factors* | |
| **F Ratios** | 0.3279 (NS) | 16.7120 * | 13.653 * | 2.5926 (NS) | 1.5969 (NS) |

* Significant at 5% level.

NS— Not Significant.

Excepting stressors from group factors and organisational role factors all the other stressors have emerged as insignificant, proving the fact that employees with different levels of salary are significantly different from each other with respect to two types of stressors only. Employees with higher salary have greater role with more assignments and so their stress sources will differ from those with lower salary. Individual factors and extra organisational factors do not cause difference in the employees with different salaries in respect of stressors.

## Type of Bank and Sources of Stress

In order to understand whether stressors differ according to the type of bank where the employees are working, Analysis of Variance has been performed and the following null hypothesis has been tested.

*Null Hypothesis:* There is no significant difference between employees belonging to the two types of banks with respect to sources of stress.

The summary of ANOVA 'F' ratios for causes of stress and type of bank has been furnished in Table 4.40.

**Table 4.40**

**Summary of ANOVA 'F' Ratios for Causes of Stress with Respect to Type of Bank**

| *Causes* | *1* | *2* | *3* | | *4* |
|---|---|---|---|---|---|
| | *Individual Factors* | *Group Factors* | *Organisational Factors* | | *Extra Organisational Factors* |
| | | | *Role Factors* | *Job Factors* | |
| **F Ratios** | 0.2299 (NS) | 0.8538 (NS) | 0.0723 (NS) | 0.2242 (NS) | 0.0323 (NS) |

NS— Not Significant.

The 'F' ratios of ANOVA performed to test whether stressors differ according to the type of bank reveals insignificant results. Hence, the null hypothesis is accepted. From the above it is understood that individual factors, group factors, role factors, job factors and extra organisational factors causing job stress do not differ according to the type of bank.

**Nature of Job (Designation) and Sources of Stress**

In order to understand the relationship between the nature of job and sources of stress, Analysis of Variance has been performed. The following null hypothesis is tested.

*Null Hypothesis:* There is no significant difference among employees of different designations with respect to stressors.

Table 4.41 shows the summary of ANOVA 'F' ratios for sources of stress with respect to nature of job.

Table 4.41

**Summary of ANOVA 'F' Ratios for Causes of Stress with Respect to Nature of Job**

| *Causes* | *1* | *2* | *3* | | *4* |
|---|---|---|---|---|---|
| | *Individual Factors* | *Group Factors* | *Organisational Factors* | | *Extra Organisational Factors* |
| | | | *Role Factors* | *Job Factors* | |
| **F Ratios** | 3.7253 (NS) | 3.0564 (NS) | 24.4170 * | 6.3560 * | 0.2007 (NS) |

* Significant at 5% level.

NS— Not Significant.

Table 4.41 clearly shows that stress caused by organisational factors such as role and job factors differ significantly among employees with respect to nature of their job. The reasons for the differences arise due to the fact that tasks to be performed and responsibility differ according to the nature of job. Stressors from other sources such as individual factors, group factors and extra organisational factors do not have significant differences for employees whose nature of job differs. Hence, the null hypothesis is accepted for individual factors, group factors and extra organisational factors and rejected for role and job factors.

**Length of Service and Sources of Stress**

In this part of the study, an attempt has been made to measure the relationship between length of service of the bank employees and sources of stress. The following null hypothesis has been framed to test the significance of relationship between length of service and sources of stress.

*Null Hypothesis:* There is no significant difference among employees of different levels of experience with respect to stressors.

Table 4.42

**Summary of ANOVA 'F' Ratios for Causes of Stress with Respect to Length of Service**

| | 1 | 2 | 3 | | 4 |
|---|---|---|---|---|---|
| *Causes* | *Individual Factors* | *Group Factors* | *Organisational Factors* | | *Extra Organisational Factors* |
| | | | *Role Factors* | *Job Factors* | |
| **F Ratios** | 2.464208 (NS) | 0.268425 (NS) | 0.82738 (NS) | 0.727406 (NS) | 2.585216 (NS) |

NS— Not Significant.

Table 4.42 reveals that all the sources of stress are non-significant, indicating thereby no significant difference among employees having different periods of service, with respect to stressors.

*Discrimination Analysis*

The next part of the study analyses the stressors that discriminate the high stress and low stress groups of bank employees. For this purpose, Discriminant Function Analysis has been used.

A linear combination of predictor variables were weighted in such a way that it will best discriminate among groups with the least error. The linear discriminant function is given by

$D = L_1X_1 + L_2X_2 \ldots\ldots\ldots\ldots\ldots\ldots + L_nX_n$ where $X_i$'s are predictor variables, $L_i$'s represent the discriminant co-efficients and D is the value of the discriminant function of a particular variable/element such that if this value is greater than a certain critical value $D^*$ the variable would be classified in group I; otherwise the variable would be classified in group II.

**Predictor Variables**

Using all the 30 statements namely B1, B2, . . . . and B30, Discriminant Analysis is performed. The final model includes 13 statements namely B1, B8, B9, B11, B14, B16, B17, B18, B19, B20, B28, B29 and B30 for discriminating between the low job stress group and high job stress group.

The respondents were classified into two groups such as high and low stress groups based on the stress scores. Respondents with stress scores above the mean score were classified under high stress group. Respondents whose stress scores were below the mean score were brought under low stress group.

Table 4.43 shows the group means of each independent variable identified for analysis as low stress and high stress groups. Test of equality of group means (univariate ANOVA) are given in Table 4.44.

**Table 4.43**

**Mean Score of Statements Among Bank Employees Groups**

| *S. No.* | *St. No.* | *Statements* | *Stress mean score* | |
|---|---|---|---|---|
| | | | *Below average* ($N_1$=199) | *Above average* ($N_2$=201) |
| 1. | B1 | INDIVIDUAL FACTOR<br>I maintain cordial relationship with co-workers (Personality trait) | 1.3216 | 1.5274 |
| 2. | B8 | GROUP FACTOR<br>I feel that the leadership in our organisation is inappropriate (Lack of leadership support) | 1.8995 | 3.1045 |
| | B9 | My superiors behaviour is inconsiderate (Poor relation with colleagues, subordinates and superiors) | 1.8291 | 3.2040 |
| | B28 | Inter-group and Intra-group conflicts in the organisation disrupts me often (Lack of group cohesiveness) | 2.3266 | 3.3881 |
| 3. | B11 | ORGANISATIONAL – JOB FACTOR<br>There is no avenue for two-way communication in our organisation (Role stagnation). | 2.1960 | 3.4527 |

(*Contd...*)

| *S. No.* | *St. No.* | *Statements* | *Stress mean score* | |
|---|---|---|---|---|
| | | | *Below average* ($N_1$=199) | *Above average* ($N_2$=201) |
| | B14 | I work under extreme time pressure (Role Overload). | 2.8894 | 4.0100 |
| | B17 | My working hours are inconvenient (Role Overload) | 1.7136 | 3.0896 |
| | B29 | My responsibilities are poorly defined which leads to clash of interests (Role Ambiguity) | 1.6030 | 2.7413 |
| | B19 | Opportunities for learning and rise in my career are fewer (Role Stagnation) | 2.0754 | 3.3731 |
| | B16 | ORGANISATIONAL–JOB FACTOR<br>I feel insignificant and powerless in the organisation (Feeling of inequity) | 1.8995 | 2.8905 |
| | B18 | I feel that my salary is less in comparison with the quantity of my labour (Feeling of paid low) | 2.1357 | 3.5224 |
| | B20 | There is no match between my abilities and the requirements of my job (Mismatch between capability of the individuals and requirements of the job) | 1.9548 | 3.1692 |
| 4. | B30 | EXTRA ORGANISATIONAL FACTOR<br>The following non-work environment had a negative influence on my job (Life crisis)<br>i. Family relocation<br>ii. Financial problems<br>iii. Illness of my family members | 1.6633 | 3.0597 |

Table 4.44

Test of Equality of Group Means - Univariate ANOVA

| *Statement No.* | *Wilk's Lembda* | *F (D=1,398)* | **P* |
|---|---|---|---|
| B1 | 0.973 | 10.975 | 0.000 |
| B8 | 0.706 | 165.676 | 0.000 |
| B9 | 0.616 | 248.415 | 0.000 |
| B11 | 0.760 | 125.932 | 0.000 |
| B14 | 0.797 | 101.656 | 0.000 |
| B16 | 0.760 | 125.456 | 0.000 |
| B17 | 0.690 | 178.959 | 0.000 |
| B18 | 0.741 | 138.774 | 0.000 |
| B19 | 0.717 | 157.018 | 0.000 |
| B20 | 0.726 | 150.169 | 0.000 |
| B28 | 0.894 | 47.124 | 0.000 |
| B29 | 0.856 | 66.954 | 0.000 |
| B30 | 0.813 | 91.543 | 0.000 |

* Significant.

**The Discriminant Function Fitted**

D = -6.381 + 0.231 B1 + 0.209 B8 + 0.334 B9 + 0.180 B11

\+

0.218 B14 + 0.205 B16 + 0.153 B17 + 0.165 B18 + 0.171 B19 + 0.195 B20 + 0.132 B 28 + 0.104 B29 + 0.222 B30

Table 4.45

Summary of Discriminant Function

| *Eigen Value* | *Wilk's Lambda* | *Chi square* | *D.F.* | *P* |
|---|---|---|---|---|
| 2.113 | .321 | 444.58 | 13 | .000 |

Using the discrminant function fitted and the observed predictor variables, the employees are classified and the correct percentage of classification is presented in Table 4.46.

### Table 4.46

### Determination of Percentage of Correct Classification by Using Discriminant Function of the Data

| *Stress* | *Classified using the fitted disfunction* | | *Total* |
|---|---|---|---|
| | *Below average* | *Above average* | |
| Below Average | 193 | 6 | 199 |
| Above average | 13 | 188 | 201 |

From Table 4.46, it is observed that out of the 400 respondents under study, 387 respondents were correctly classified. Hence, the percentage of correct classification is (381/400)*100 or 95.3%.

## Results of Overall Step-wise Discriminant Analysis

The results of the overall step-wise discriminant analysis and discriminant functions obtained and the test of significance are given in Table 4.47. It shows that four factors, viz., Group factors, Organisational role factors, Organisational job factors and extra organisational factors have major differences between high stress and low stress groups of bank employees.

### Table 4.47

### Canonical Discriminant Function Co-efficient

| *S. No.* | *Factors* | *Function co-efficient* |
|---|---|---|
| 1. | Group Factor (My superiors' behaviour is inconsiderate) | 1.3749 |
| 2. | Organisational – Role Factor (My working hours are inconvenient) | 1.376 |
| 3. | Organisational – Job Factor (I feel that my salary is less in comparison with the quality of my labour) | 1.3867 |
| 4. | Extra-organisational Factor (The following non-work environment had a negative influence on my job:<br>i. Family relocation<br>ii. Financial problems<br>iii. Illness of my family members | 1.3964 |

**Relative Importance of Predictor Variables**

The relative importance of each predictor variables in discriminating between the two groups are obtained using the formula given and the results are presented below:

Formula:

Ij = I Kj (Xj1-Xj2)I

Where, Ij = Importance value of $j^{th}$ characters

Kj = Unstandardised discriminant co-efficient for the $j^{th}$ characters

Xjk = Mean of the $j^{th}$ character for the $k^{th}$ group and

Rj = Relative importance of the $j^{th}$ character

Table 4.48 shows the relative importance of factors in discriminating between the groups.

**Table 4.48**

**Relative Importance of Statements in Discriminating Between the Groups**

| *Statement No.* | *Ij* | *Relative Importance (%)* |
|---|---|---|
| B1 | 0.0475 | 1.28 |
| B8 | 0.2105 | 7.25 |
| B9 | 0.2443 | 8.441 |
| B11 | 0.2262 | 7.79 |
| B14 | 0.2288 | 7.88 |
| B16 | 0.2032 | 6.99 |
| B17 | 0.2518 | 8.67 |
| B18 | 0.3167 | 10.90 |
| B19 | 0.2219 | 7.64 |
| B20 | 0.2368 | 8.15 |
| B28 | 0.1401 | 4.82 |
| B29 | 0.1184 | 4.07 |
| B30 | 0.4592 | 15.80 |
| **Total** | **2.9055** | **100.00** |

The relative importance percentage gives the contribution of each variable to discriminant function of the 13 factors discriminating between high stress and low stress group. Extra organisational factor (St. No. B30) contributes more followed by the organisational – job factor (St. No. B18). The third and fourth factors which discriminate between the groups are 'organisational – role factor' and 'group factor'. (B17 and B9)

## OBJECTIVE 5

The fifth objective of the present study is 'to understand the relationship between individuals' "personality type" and their stress managing ability'. In this part of the study, analysis related to the above stated objective has been made. Correlation analysis has been applied to study the relationship between personality type and stress management ability of the select bank employees.

### *Stress Management Ability*

The stress management ability has been measured based on the responses to the statements such as 'My feeling of tension increases in stressful situation', 'I can accept changes in work as normal', I have difficulty in coping with situations' and 'I can manage hectic situations'.

### *Personality Type*

Personality is the most important determinant of stress. Each and every individual possesses a personality of his own. The personality types are categorised into *A*, *B* and *AB*.

Type *A* has the following characteristics:

- Intensely competitive;
- Impatient;
- Achievement oriented;
- Aggressive;
- Having a distorted sense of time urgency;
- Moving rapidly and frequently;
- Talking fast and listening impatiently.

Type *B* personality has the following characteristics:

- Relaxed and unhurried;
- Patient;
- Non-competitive;
- Non-aggressive;
- Not having time urgency.

The *AB* type personality is the mixture of both *A* and *B* type personality. The sampled respondents possess the characteristics of both *A* and *B* type personality traits and *AB*. The employees with *A* type personality are rigid and determined and the employees with *B* type personality are a bit patient and less competitive.

**Analysis and Interpretation of the Data Regarding Personality Type of the Employees**

In this section, the data on personality type of the employees is reported according to their cadre. The cadre of the employees has been divided into managerial and non-managerial. Those who are in the designation of managers and assistant managers are categorised as managerial and the employees below the rank of assistant manager are termed as non-managerial for the purpose of this study.

Table 4.49 shows the distribution of managerial personnel according to personality type.

**Table 4.49**

**Distribution of Managerial Personnel According to Personality Type**

| *Personality* | *Total* | *Percentage* |
|---|---|---|
| Type A | 2 | 1.20 |
| Type B | 7 | 4.22 |
| Type AB | 157 | 94.58 |
| **Total** | **166** | **100.00** |

The results reported in Table 4.49 revealed that out of 166 managerial personnel studied, 157 (94.58 per cent) fall in *AB* type personality. They possess the characteristics of both *A* and *B* personality. Among the managerial personnel, 7 (4.22 per cent) fall in *B* type personality. They are patient, less competitive and non/aggressive in performing their jobs. The remaining 2 managerial personnel (1.20 per cent) fall in the *A* type personality. These employees are aggressive and competitive with high self esteem.

### Distribution of Non-Managerial Personnel According to Personality Type

Table 4.50 presents the distribution of non-managerial personnel according to their personality type such as type *A*, type *B* and type *AB*.

Table 4.50

Distribution of Non-Managerial Personnel According to Personality Type

| *Personality* | *Total* | *Percentage* |
|---|---|---|
| Type A | 6 | 2.56 |
| Type B | 6 | 2.56 |
| Type AB | 222 | 94.88 |
| **Total** | **234** | **100.00** |

It is observed from Table 4.50 that out of 234 non-managerial personnel studied, 222 (94.88 per cent) fall in *AB* type personality. They possess the characteristics of both *A* and *B* personality. Among the non-managerial personnel, 6 (2.56 per cent) fall in *B* type personality. They are patient, relatively less competitive and non-aggressive in performing their jobs. The remaining 6 non-managerial personnel (2.56 per cent) fall in the *A* type personality. These employees are aggressive and competitive with high self esteem.

## Analysis and Interpretation of the Data Regarding Stress Management Ability

In this section, the data on stress management ability of the employees is reported. The stress management/resistance ability has been measured as good, fair and poor. The employees have been classified into three groups according to the stress management ability. The scores for stress management ability of select bank employees ranged from 5 to 12. The respondents, whose scores were 11 and above, were classified as having good stress management ability. The respondents who had scored more than 7 but less than 11 were treated as fairly stress manageable persons, while the others were categorised as having poor stress management ability.

Table 4.51 shows the distribution of managerial personnel according to their stress management ability.

**Table 4.51**

**Distribution of Managerial Personnel According to Stress Management Ability**

| *Stress Management Ability* | *Total* | *Percentage* |
|---|---|---|
| Good | 7 | 4.22 |
| Fair | 90 | 54.22 |
| Poor | 69 | 41.56 |
| **Total** | **166** | **100.00** |

The results reported in Table 4.51 implies that out of 166 executives studied, 69 (41.56 per cent) fall in poor stress management ability category. They are less efficient in managing occupational stress. 54.22 per cent of the sampled employees' stress management ability is fair. These employees possess stress management ability to a certain extent. However, in case of heavy strain, these employees may not be able to manage. The remaining 7 (4.22 per cent) have good stress management ability. These employees are good at combating stress under any circumstance. Considering the whole managerial personnel, only lower percentage (4.22 per cent) is capable of resisting their occupational stress. It reveals that other managerial personnel need motivation and training to cope up with occupational stress.

**Distribution of Non-Managerial Personnel According to Stress Management Ability**

Table 4.52 shows the distribution of non-managerial personnel according to their stress management ability. Three classifications such as good, fair or poor stress managing ability were made here based on the scores.

Table 4.52

**Distribution of Non-Managerial Personnel According to Stress Management Ability**

| *Stress Management Ability* | *Total* | *Percentage* |
|---|---|---|
| Good | 15 | 6.41 |
| Fair | 150 | 64.10 |
| Poor | 69 | 29.49 |
| **Total** | **234** | **100.00** |

The results presented in Table 4.52 show that out of 234 non-managerial personnel studied, 69 (29.49 per cent) possess poor stress management ability. They have difficulty in dealing with stressful situations and feel uncomfortable under stressful situations. 64.1 per cent of the sampled non-managerial personnel had fair level of stress management ability.

They are able to manage the occupational stress most of the times but not always. The remaining 15 (6.41 per cent) possess good stress management ability. They are successful in performing their jobs in spite of experiencing occupational stress.

**Correlation Between Personality Type and Stress Management Ability**

Correlation between personality type and stress management ability of the employees (managerial and non-managerial personnel) is discussed below. Table 4.53 shows the co-efficient of correlation between the personality type *A* and the stress management ability of the employees.

**Table 4.53**

**Correlation Co-efficient Between the Personality Type A and Stress Management Ability**

| *Category* | *Total* | *r* |
|---|---|---|
| Managerial | 2 | 0.245 |
| Non-managerial | 6 | 0.137 |

To study the degree of relationship between personality type and stress management ability of managerial and non-managerial personnel, correlation co-efficient was found out. It was found that personality type *A* and stress management ability of managerial personnel was positively correlated (r = 0.245) but negligible.

The correlation coefficient between personality type *A* and stress management ability of non-managerial personnel also denotes that the degree of association between personality type and stress management ability is low. In both the cases, i.e., managerial and non-managerial personnel, the relationship between personality type and stress management ability is not significant. Hence, it may be concluded that the degree of correlation between personality type '*A*' and the stress management ability is low in the case of both managerial and non-managerial cadres.

### Correlation Co-Efficient Between the Personality Type *B* and Stress Management Ability

Table 4.54 shows the correlation coefficient between the Personality Type *B* and stress management ability.

Table 4.54

**Correlation Co-efficient Between the Personality Type *B* and Stress Management Ability**

| *Category* | *Total* | *r* |
|---|---|---|
| Managerial | 7 | 0.954 |
| Non-managerial | 6 | 0.022 |

The analysis revealed that the degree of correlation between personality type *B* and stress management ability of managerial personnel is positive and high. In the case of non-managerial, the correlation co-efficient is positive but negligible. It implies that the stress management ability of managerial personnel in type *B* category is significantly related with the personality type. Higher the politeness, less competitive and non-aggressive, higher is the stress resistance.

### Correlation Co-Efficient Between the Personality Type *AB* and Stress Management Ability

Table 4.55 presents the correlation coefficient between the Personality Type *AB* and stress management ability.

Table 4.55

Correlation Co-efficient Between the Personality Type AB and Stress Management Ability

| *Category* | *Total* | *r* |
|---|---|---|
| Managerial | 157 | 0.954 |
| Non-managerial | 222 | 0.191 |

The analysis revealed that the correlation between personality type *AB* and stress management ability of managerial personnel is positive and significant. In the case of non-managerial employees, the correlation co-efficient is positive but low. It implies that there is a high degree of positive correlation between personality type *AB* and stress management ability in the case of managerial cadre and low degree of correlation in the case of non-managerial personnel.

From the analysis made, it may be concluded that a combination of the characteristics of personality Type *A* and personality Type *B* influences the way, the bank employees of the managerial category manage their stress.

**OBJECTIVE 6**

The sixth objective of the study is to analyse the effects of job stress on the individuals and on the organisation. Excessive job stress has been widely recognised as a source of increased discontent with job of an individual. Although stress is considered necessary for personal growth, change, development and performance, it does put a strain on the individual.

Physiological stress symptoms may include headaches, high blood pressure and/or an acid stomach. Psychological responses may include apathy, forgetfulness, irritability or dissatisfaction. Individual behavioural consequences may include loss of appetite, weight gain or loss, change in tobacco or alcohol habits or sudden alterations in appearance. An individual's response to stressors will be mediated somewhat by his or her personality characteristics.

The problems due to high levels of stress can be exhibited physically, psychologically or behaviourally by the individual. Stress can cause depression, inhibition, anxiety, fatigue, lowered self-esteem and reduced job satisfaction.

Stress takes a toll on the body and the mind. Long term and short term stress have the same effects. They include decreased energy, decreased concentration, more negative emotions, difficulty with relationships, and accelerated ageing. People under great amounts of stress not only feel but look tired. They are drained and usually unwilling to participate in anything physically straining. Concentration levels decrease as stress levels increase. One cannot concentrate when he has a million things already on his mind.

When a person feels he is "under the gun," he is much more likely to show his negative side. He becomes very pessimistic about himself and others. Since it is so hard to focus when under stress, the relationships, work related, family or personal, suffer greatly. Stress affects the body by increasing signs of ageing.

In addition, events that are very stressful to one person may not be stressful to another; individuals vary in the amount of stress they can tolerate without showing signs of job-related tension. This section of the study analyses the effects of job stress on individuals and on the organisation as a whole.

### Individual Level Effects

At the individual level, stress is responsible for psychosomatic outcomes such as psychiatric disorders, heart disease, high blood pressure, and illness behaviours. Researches have shown that negative effects such as anxiety and depression caused by stress and behavioural coping responses such as poor health practices, less sleep, and increased smoking and drinking, may influence the immune system of an individual.

Today, people experience stressors which are very different from those early survival ones. Yet positive stressors such as getting married, or negative stressors such as family conflicts, still cause the same physiological fight or flight response.

### Weighted Average Analysis of Individual Effects

The consequence of occupational stress results in personal and organisational problems. The adverse individual effects and organisational effects have been analysed separately. The individual effects include making the employees completely exhausted, irritation, nervousness, anger and dissatisfaction on the job.

People suffering from excessive stress may not be able to concentrate on their work and their performance will be poor. Stress is also the root cause of anxiety, which ultimately affects the normal psychological responses of human beings, resulting in tension and fatigue. Excessive stress also results in job dissatisfaction. Negative feeling resulting from job stress reduces stress resistance. Such kind of deficiency results in less job involvement and intention to quit the job.

On the other hand, there may be some advantageous effects, which include calmness and relaxation at work, doing the work in the best possible way and considering the official assignments as more important than the personal interests. These effects have been analysed with weighted average analysis based on the research study conducted on job stress by J.T. Walsh and Taber (1974). The variables are measured on a five point agree-disagree scale. The weighted average scores are presented in Table 4.56.

**Table 4.56**

**Weighted Average Analysis of Individual Effects**

| *Sl. No.* | *Effects on individuals* | | *Weighted average score* |
|---|---|---|---|
| | *Type of Effect* | *Statements* | |
| E8 | No Intention to quit | I have not thought of quitting my job | 4.28 |
| E9 | Job involvement | I feel that my official assignments are more important than my personal interests | 4.22 |
| E5 | No Anxiety | I always feel calm and relaxed at work | 3.66 |
| E1 | Fatigue | I feel completely exhausted at the end of the day at my office | 3.12 |
| E2 | Tension | I look irritated, nervous, angry and tensed while performing my job | 2.14 |
| E4 | Job Dissatisfaction | I feel dissatisfied with my job | 1.96 |

It is evident from Table 4.56 that advantageous effects are more than the adverse effects of occupational stress on the employees. Though the employees have been facing stressful situation in their everyday work, they do not have intention to quit the job. They also give much importance to their official assignments than to their personal interests.

Bank employees do not seem to suffer from much tension, since the weighted average score is 2.14 which indicate that they disagree to the statement which measures the existence of tension. However, the weighted average mean of 3.12 for statement E1 aimed at measuring the presence of fatigue in the job, indicates that they more or less agree, though not strongly with this statement. Employees do not experience anxiety in their jobs as they agree to feel calm and relaxed at work as is evident from the high weighted mean score of 3.66. Job dissatisfaction due to occupational stress among bank employees is found low as is evident from the lowest weighted score of 1.96.

### *Organisational Level Effects*

At the organisational level, researches have shown that work-related stresses may be responsible for organisational outcomes such as decline in performance, less commitment, increase in absenteeism and turnover, increasing employee conflicts and lower productivity.

Stress may have a positive or negative impact on performance and on the quantity of work done. When employees start feeling moderate levels of stress, their efforts towards work and performance may increase. However, if stress becomes too high or persists for a long time, the efforts put in by them decreases resulting in increased labour turnover and absenteeism.

The quality of work done by the individual also gets affected if a person experiencing stress pre-occupies himself with routine work without channelising his efforts for the achievement of the goals of the organisation.

### *Weighted Average Analysis of Organisational Effects*

Effect on quantity of work, quality of work and absenteeism are the variables measuring effect of occupational stress on banks which are measured on a five point agree-disagree scale.

Table 4.57 shows the weighted average scores of organisational effects of job stress (effects on bank).

Table 4.57

Weighted Average Analysis of Organisational Effects

| *St. No.* | *Organisational Effects* | | *Weighted average score* |
|---|---|---|---|
| | *Type of effect* | *Statements* | |
| E7 | Effect on quantity of work | I am not able to complete my work in the stipulated time | 2.49 |
| E3 | Effect on quality of work | I feel that I am not doing my job in the best way | 1.94 |
| E6 | Absenteeism | I have taken a number of days of leave due to severe stress | 1.82 |

It is understood from Table 4.57 that the quantity of work done by employees gets affected since the weighted average of 2.49 indicates that bank employees agree to the statement E7. The second effect of job stress on bank is on the quality of work (weighted average score 1.94). This may be due to the fact that the nature of bank jobs are such that they are more time bound and so employees concentrate on finishing the job within the time deadline. Thus quality of work gets affected. This may also be due to the reason that bank employees experience fatique which results in poor quality of work. However, employees' presence for work is not much affected by stress. The lowest weighted average score of 1.82 for number of days of leave taken indicating lower absenteeism substantiates this observation.

## OBJECTIVES 7 AND 8

The seventh and eighth objectives of the study are: to examine the significant stress coping strategies adopted by bank employees and to analyse the relationship between demographic and job related variables and level of adoption of stress coping strategies. The coping strategies adopted may be individual or organisational. In this study, both the individual strategies as well organisational strategies have been analysed. After identifying the coping strategies, factor analysis has been used to examine the most effective coping strategy followed by the bank employees. The relationship between demographic and job related variables and the stress coping strategies has been analysed by performing analysis of variance (ANOVA).

### *Coping Strategies*

Individuals cannot remain in a continuous state of tension. They adopt different ways of dealing with stress which is called coping. Coping strategies refer to the specific efforts, both behavioural and psychological, that people employ to minimise stressful events. Coping with stress begins with learning to give oneself permission to be happy. Some people play the part of a victim, insisting other people to make them feel stressed.

Literature on stress states that coping strategies may be classified as individual strategies and organisational strategies. Individual strategies include 'work-focussed' coping strategies and 'emotion-focussed' ccoping strategies. Organisational strategies comprise of health maintenance programmes, leadership training programmes and stress reduction workshops.

### Work-focussed Coping Strategies

Some of the work-focussed coping strategies are role clarification, time management, delegation and co-operative work.

Role clarification refers to clarification sought by employees from their superiors in case of ambiguity in role description. Proper time management can be done to organise work more effectively. Delegation of work to subordinates reduces work overload with the resultant effect on reducing job stress.

Co-operating with other employees by sharing information and dividing work is an effective way of reducing stress.

### Emotional-Focussed Coping Strategies

These are the second set of individual based coping strategies. These strategies help employees adjust to stress more easily. Increased social support, tolerance, relaxation techniques, health maintenance and reduced perfectionism are some of the emotion-focussed strategies of coping with stress.

Supportive colleagues and friends provide the social support to reduce stress.

Role ambiguity cannot be reduced in many work situations. Under such circumstances tolerance in the work helps to reduce stress.

Doing yoga and meditation, and other forms of physical exercises help to reduce tension. Health maintenance through a balanced diet and enough sleep helps in shaping the body better to deal with stress.

Attempts by people to live up to the impossible standards set make them stressful. In such a situation, a better way of reducing stress is by learning to live with reduced perfectionism.

Apart from the individual stress coping strategies, organisations have many programmes to help employees to deal with stress. Such programmes include Health maintenance by offering gym facilities, leadership training, counselling and listening to employees' problems. Stress reduction workshops are also organised for employees.

*Factor Analysis*

Factor analysis has been used to identify the most effective coping strategy followed by the bank employees. Questions for measuring the coping strategies adopted by the sampled respondents were framed based on the scales developed by Dew and Guest, 1989. Responses to the 24 questions were collected on a three point scale and the data so collected (n=400) were subjected to Principal Component Analysis with Varimax rotation, to identify the dimensions of coping strategies adopted by the bank employees.

For interpretation of factors, factor loadings greater than 0.38 is considered to be significant (Harman, 1976). Eight factors accounting for a total of 61.7 percentage of the variance have been obtained. These obtained factors are used as variables for further analysis and interpretation.

The results of factor analysis for coping strategies are presented below:

The first factor extracted a variance of 9.97 per cent of the total variance. It can be noted from Table 4.58 that the factor has got significant loadings on 'Statements 7 and 8'. This indicates that rational task oriented behaviour is one of the coping strategies adopted by the bank employees. 'Statements 16, 20 and 18' denote that instant reaction and emotional relief are also coping strategies followed by the bank employees. Therefore, this factor is named as *"Rational Task Oriented Behaviour and Instant Reaction"*

Table 4.58

Significant Loadings of Variables on Varimax Factor I

| *St. No.* | *Statement* | *Loadings* |
|---|---|---|
| F 7 | Setting priorities | 0.764 |
| F 8 | Finding out more about the situation | 0.731 |
| F 16 | Taking immediate action to reduce the effect of a stressful situation | 0.594 |
| F 20 | Accepting oneself what is happening | 0.557 |
| F 18 | Keeping quiet and cool | 0.489 |

Factor I indicates that in order to reduce the stress, priority has been set for the work and the situation was properly understood by the employees. In case of stressful situation, immediate action is to be taken in order to reduce the stress. The employees have to understand themselves and the surroundings. The impact of stress is also avoided by simply keeping quiet and cool.

This coping strategy is a work focussed strategy, whereby employees could reduce stress by changing their work habits and getting assistance and finding out more information which will reduce anxiety about the work.

Table 4.59 shows the factor loadings on Factor II. It is constituted by 'Statements 2, 1 and 3'. The factor loadings on these statements account for about 9.91 per cent of the total variance.

Table 4.59

Significant Loadings of Variables on Varimax Factor II

| *St. No.* | *Statement* | *Loadings* |
|---|---|---|
| F 2 | Do meditation | 0.852 |
| F 1 | Practicing yoga | 0.845 |
| F 3 | Do physical exercises | 0.733 |
| F 4 | Have creative pastimes like music and hobbies | 0.617 |

This factor indicates that doing meditation, yoga and physical exercises have helped employees to get rid of stress. Yoga and supernatural meditation have been in use since ancient times as the techniques of relief from stress and for improvement in physical and psychological health. If the stressful situation cannot be changed then one has to try to cope with it. Coping with stress can be effective by closing the eyes, or by doing physical exercises and yoga. Very high positive loadings on 'Statements 2, 1, 3 and 4' indicate that doing meditation, practicing yoga, doing physical exercises and having creative pastimes have been very effective in getting relief from stressful situation in the case of the sampled respondents and it is a healthy way of coping with job stress and an emotion-focussed coping strategy. Hence, this factor is named as *"Relief Techniques"*.

The third factor extracted a variance of 8.71 per cent of the total variations. This factor has obtained high positive factor loadings on 'Statements 24, 23 and 22' as detailed below in Table 4.60.

**Table 4.60**

**Significant Loadings of Variables on Varimax Factor III**

| *St. No.* | *Statement* | *Loadings* |
|---|---|---|
| F 24 | Stress reduction workshops organised for the employees | 0.860 |
| F 23 | Leadership training programmes for better counselling and listening to employees problems | 0.821 |
| F 22 | Health maintenance programmes in the organisation like gym facilities | 0.680 |

High positive factor loading on 'Statements 24, 23 and 22' indicate that in order to reduce the job stress among employees, initiatives have been taken at the organisational level. The situations which cause or are likely to cause stress to the employees could be prevented by adopting certain precautionary and corrective interventions at organisational level. These measures include conducting of stress reduction workshops, leadership training programmes and health maintenance programmes by the banks. This factor is thus named as *"Organisational Strategies"*.

The fourth factor extracted a variation of 8.55 per cent of the total variations. Table 4.61 shows the factor loadings on the 'Statements 13, 14, 12 and 15'.

**Table 4.61**

**Significant Loadings of Variables on Varimax Factor IV**

| *St. No.* | *Statement* | *Loadings* |
|---|---|---|
| F 13 | Leave the office early with permission | 0.779 |
| F 14 | Take a day off | 0.731 |
| F 12 | Express irritability to self | 0.573 |
| F 15 | Take rest and feel fresh | 0.490 |

High positive loadings on 'Statements 13, 14, 12 and 15' indicate that one has to prepare himself to face the stressors. It is clear from the factor loadings that allotting time to think things over and sort out the problems by leaving early and taking a day off had been resorted to by employees to reduce stress. Preparation to face the stressful situation included taking rest and also expressing the irritability to self. Based on this interpretation, the factor is termed as *"Strategies of Preparation"*.

Table 4.62 shows the factor loadings on Factor V constituted by 'Statements 11 and 4'. The variations on this factor accounts for 6.61 per cent of the total variations.

**Table 4.62**

**Significant Loadings of Variables on Varimax Factor V**

| *St. No.* | *Statement* | *Loadings* |
|---|---|---|
| F 11 | Forget about the problem | 0.641 |

High positive loadings on 'Statement 11' describes that stress could be reduced by the employees by diverting their attention by forgetting the problem. This is an effective coping strategy and thus this factor is named as *"Distraction Technique"*.

The sixth factor extracted a variation of 6.59 per cent of the total variations. The 'Statements 10 and 9' constituted the sixth factor. Table 4.63 presents the factor loadings on these statements.

**Table 4.63**

**Significant Loadings of Variables on Varimax Factor VI**

| *St. No.* | *Statement* | *Loadings* |
|---|---|---|
| F 10 | Letting the feeling wear off | 0.748 |
| F 9 | Take some work home | 0.701 |

High positive loadings on 'Statement 10' signify that to manage the occupational stress, it is better to keep the stressful event away for some time. This kind of approach expects that circumstances will bring about the solution to the problem. Working on the job at home to ease a stressful situation also alleviates stress as seen from the high factor loading for 'Statement 9', Based on the above interpretation, this factor is named as "*Impersistive approach*".

The significant loadings obtained on different statements of factor VII are presented in Table 4.64. The seventh factor extracted a variation of 5.93 per cent of the total variations.

**Table 4.64**

**Significant Loadings of Variables on Varimax Factor VII**

| *St. No.* | *Statement* | *Loadings* |
|---|---|---|
| F 6 | Consulting friends in solving problems | 0.702 |
| F 5 | Discussing official problems with family members | 0.691 |
| F 17 | Emotional outburst | 0.484 |

High positive loadings on 'Statements 6, 5 and 17' indicate that stress management techniques adopted by the bank employees include support from family and friends. In the event of stressful situation, one can expect the support from family members and friends. Sounding out work-related problems to family members seems to act as an efficient coping measure as seen from the high loadings on statement F5. Several research studies have proved that social support has a pre-dominant role in bringing down the effects of stressful situations (Sarason I.G., Levine H.M., 1983).

Hence, this factor is named as *"Eliciting Social Support"*.

The eighth factor extracted a variance of 5.43 per cent of the total variations. The positive loadings on 'Statements 19 and 21' show that a stressful situation should be tackled immediately. Table 4.65 shows the factor loadings on these statements.

**Table 4.65**

**Significant Loadings of Variables on Varimax Factor VIII**

| *St. No.* | *Statement* | *Loadings* |
|---|---|---|
| F 19 | Ignoring the problem | 0.699 |
| F 21 | Expecting superiors support | 0.541 |

Positive loadings on 'Statements 19 and 21' reveal that acting submissively with the superiors and others are strategies adopted to reduce stress. Ignoring the problem that caused the stress has also been a successful strategy. When a person expects support from his superiors, he endures the stressful situation. It can give him relief from the stress. High positive loadings on these statements denote that bank employees follow such passive attempts. Hence, this factor is named as *"Passive attempts"*.

***Weighted Average Analysis of Coping Strategies***

The bank employees have adopted different coping strategies to reduce their occupational stress. In order to ascertain the most effective coping strategy, from among the various strategies adopted, weighted average analysis has been made.

For this purpose the coping strategies adopted by the employees have been grouped into 9 classes, as already stated viz., Relaxation Techniques, Strategies of preparations, Elicitation of social support, Distraction Techniques, Rational

Task Oriented behaviour, Passive attempts, Emotional Relief, Instant Reaction and Organisational Strategies. Table 4.66 shows the weighted average score to each of the types of coping strategies shown above.

**Table 4.66**

**Weighted Average Analysis of Coping Strategies**

| *S. No.* | *Coping Strategies* | *Weighted average score* |
|---|---|---|
| 1. | Instant reaction (F16) | 2.203 |
| 2. | Rational Task Oriented Behaviour (F7, F8 & F9) | 2.159 |
| 3. | Emotional Relief (F17 & F18) | 2.010 |
| 4. | Passive attempts (F10, F11, F19, F20 & F21) | 1.977 |
| 5. | Elicitation of social support (F5 & F6) | 1.886 |
| 6. | Relaxation Techniques (F1, F2, F3 & F4) | 1.737 |
| 7. | Organisational Strategies (F22, F23 & F24) | 1.694 |
| 8. | Strategies of Preparations (F13, F14 & F15) | 1.513 |
| 9. | Distraction Techniques (F12) | 1.448 |

Table 4.66 reveals that Instant reaction has been the most effective coping strategy in reducing the occupational stress. The instant reaction strategy has got the highest mean score of 2.203, which implies that employees have this instant reaction which helps them to alleviate the effect of job stress. It is followed by Rational Task Oriented Behaviour with a weighted average score of 2.159. The third strategy, which is effective in coping with the stress, is Emotional Relief. However, Strategies of Preparation, and Distraction Techniques are the lesser effective strategies when compared to the other methods of coping with stress.

*Coping Strategies and Demographic Variables*

Having analysed the coping strategies adopted by bank employees, the next part of the study deals with the level of adoption of coping strategies analysed on the basis of demographic variables and job related variables. Level of adoption of coping strategies has been categorised based on the scores into three such as high (coping strategies adoption score above 56), medium (coping strategies adoption score 39 to 56) and low (coping strategies adoption score below 39). The analysis is presented in Tables numbering 4.67 to 4.87. The null hypotheses framed and tested for the purpose of analysis are stated with respect to each of the demographic and job related variables.

The first variable considered is 'Age' for which the related results are exhibited in Tables 4.67 to 4.70 along with the null hypothesis.

### Age and Level of Adoption of Coping Strategies

Table 4.67 portrays the age and the level of adoption of coping strategies.

**Table 4.67**

**Age and Level of Adoption of Coping Strategies**

| *S. No.* | *Age* | *Level of adoption of coping strategies* | | | *Total* |
|---|---|---|---|---|---|
| | | *Low* | *Medium* | *High* | |
| 1. | Below 35 years | 3 (3.9) | 53 (69.7) | 20 (26.4) | 76 |
| 2. | 36-50 years | 31 (14.4) | 153 (71.2) | 31 (14.4) | 215 |
| 3. | Above 50 years | 6 (5.5) | 84 (77.1) | 19 (17.4) | 109 |
| | **Total** | **40** | **290** | **70** | **400** |

From Table 4.67 it is observed that in all the age groups of employees, majority of the respondents have adopted medium level of coping strategies. Low level of adoption of coping strategies was found minimum in the case of employees below 35 years. Among those adopting high level of coping strategies higher percentage comprises of those below 35 years.

In order to understand whether the level of adoption of coping strategies differ among the three age groups, mean scores of adoption of coping strategies were arrived at.

The bank employees adopt different strategies for coping job stress. Table 4.68 shows the mean score of adoption of coping strategies according to their age.

**Table 4.68**

**Age and Level of Adoption of Coping Strategies – Mean Scores**

| *S. No.* | *Age group* | *No. of respondents* | *Mean score* |
|---|---|---|---|
| 1. | Below 35 years | 76 | 46.96 |
| 2. | 36-50 years | 215 | 45.23 |
| 3. | Above 50 years | 109 | 46.59 |

It is understood from Table 4.68 that the mean score of adoption of coping strategies was marginally higher among employees whose age were below 35 years. The second largest mean score of level of adoption of stress coping stress strategies was found among the age group of above 50 years. The age group between 36 and 50 years had the least mean score of adoption of stress coping strategies. It means that the young employees adopt more coping strategies than the middle aged and old employees.

*Null hypothesis:* There is no significant difference among employees belonging to the different age groups with respect to the level of adoption of coping strategies (Each coping strategy is considered individually).

Coping techniques one (Relaxation techniques), three (Elicitation of social support) and seven (Emotional relief) are significant as seen from the Table 4.69. Passive attempts and Rational task oriented behaviour may be adopted by respondents whatever be their age. The other strategies, such as 'distraction techniques' and 'instant reactions' can also be developed as coping strategies by respondents only with passage of time. In view of this explanation, the null hypothesis is rejected for coping strategies one, three and seven and accepted for the rest of the strategies.

**Table 4.69**

**Summary of ANOVA 'F' Ratios for Coping Strategies with Respect to Age**

| Coping Strategies | 1 Relaxation sechniques | 2 Strategies of preparations | 3 Elicitation of social support | 4 Distraction techniques | 5 Rational task oriented behaviour | 6 Passive attempts | 7 Emotional relief | 8 Instant reaction | 9 Organisational strategies |
|---|---|---|---|---|---|---|---|---|---|
| F Ratios | 5.7439 * | 0.6124 (NS) | 5.9272 * | 1.7528 (NS) | 1.1915 (NS) | 2.617 (NS) | 4.5095 * | 1.0634 (NS) | 0.4542 (NS) |

* Significant at 5% level.

NS— Not Significant.

**Gender and Level of Adoption of Coping Strategies**

Men and women view problems in different angles. In certain cases, men do not view the problems seriously unlike women, who take them seriously. The strategies adopted for coping with certain problems by men and women may differ from each other. Because of their nature of tolerance, women may keep on adjusting with problems. The present analysis aims at finding whether there is significant difference between male and female employees with respect to the level of adoption of coping strategies.

Table 4.70 shows the level of adoption of coping strategies by the gender groups.

From Table 4.70 it is noted that majority of the male and female respondents had adopted medium level of coping strategies. Among the employees, who had adopted high level strategies higher percentage are the male category. Higher percentage of those who had adopted low level strategies was the female employees. It is therefore understood that high level strategies were adopted more by male employees than female employees.

**Table 4.70**

**Gender and Level of Adoption of Coping Strategies**

| *S. No.* | *Gender* | *Level of adoption of coping strategies* | | | *Total* |
|---|---|---|---|---|---|
| | | *Low* | *Medium* | *High* | |
| 1. | Male | 31 (9.2) | 242 (71.8) | 64 (19.0) | 337 |
| 2. | Female | 9 (14.3) | 48 (76.2) | 6 (9.5) | 63 |
| | **Total** | **40** | **290** | **70** | **400** |

The mean scores of coping strategies adopted by the gender groups are given in Table 4.71.

**Table 4.71**

**Gender and Level of Adoption of Coping Strategies – Mean Scores**

| *S. No.* | *Gender* | *No. of respondents* | *Mean score* |
|---|---|---|---|
| 1. | Male | 337 | 46.12 |
| 2. | Female | 63 | 44.94 |

Table 4.71 reveals that the mean score of adoption of coping strategies of male employees was greater than the female employees. This shows that the male employees adopt more coping strategies than the female employees, which is the same as concluded from the previous analysis.

The significance of the difference in the level of adoption of coping strategies between male and female employees is tested here.

*Null hypothesis:* There is no significant difference between the employees belonging to the two gender groups with respect to the level of adoption of coping strategies (Each coping strategy is considered individually).

Table 4.72

Summary of ANOVA 'F' Ratios for Coping Strategies with Respect to Gender

| Coping Strategies | 1 | 2 | 3 | 4 | 5 | 6 | 7 | 8 | 9 |
|---|---|---|---|---|---|---|---|---|---|
| | *Relaxation techniques* | *Strategies of preparations* | *Elicitation of social support* | *Distraction techniques* | *Rational task oriented behaviour* | *Passive attempts* | *Emotional relief* | *Instant reaction* | *Organisational strategies* |
| **F Ratios** | 0.2041 (NS) | 1.0611 (NS) | 0.3039 (NS) | 6.23997* | 0.8188 (NS) | 1.7627 (NS) | 0.236 (NS) | 1.0729 (NS) | 8.9027* |

* Significant at 5% level.

NS— Not Significant.

Excepting coping techniques, four (Distraction techniques) and nine (Organisational Strategies), all the other techniques are not significant, as seen from the above Table. 'Passive attempts' and 'Instant reaction' are 'emotion-focussed' strategies which may be followed by the respondents irrespective of their gender. 'Strategies of Preparation' and 'Rational Task Oriented Behaviour' are either 'approach' or 'work-focussed' strategies which most probably can be developed as a coping strategy by all. In view of this explanation, the null hypothesis is rejected for coping strategies four and nine and accepted for all the other strategies.

## Educational Qualification and Level of Adoption of Coping Strategies

Education makes a man an expert in his field. Educated people possess analytical skills. It helps them to cope up with the problems. In respect of job stress, the bank employees adopt certain strategies. It is found necessary for this study whether there is any significant relationship between educational qualification and level of adoption of coping strategies.

Table 4.73

**Educational Qualification and Level of Adoption of Coping Strategies**

| *S. No.* | *Educational Qualification* | *Level of Adoption of Coping Strategies* | | | *Total* |
|---|---|---|---|---|---|
| | | *Low* | *Medium* | *High* | |
| 1. | School level | 9 (34.6) | 14 (53.9) | 3 (11.5) | 26 |
| 2. | Graduate | 15 (6.8) | 164 (74.2) | 42 (19.0) | 221 |
| 3. | Post Graduate | 16 (10.5) | 112 (73.2) | 25 (16.3) | 153 |
| | **Total** | **40** | **290** | **70** | **400** |

From Table 4.73, it is understood that higher percentage of the employees belonging to all the three educational categories had adopted medium level of coping strategies. Of those who had low level adoption of coping strategies, higher percentage are the school educated. Higher percentage of the high coping strategy group are those who are graduates.

Mean scores for the coping strategies are shown in Table 4.74.

Table 4.74

**Educational Qualification and Level of Adoption of Coping Strategies – Mean Scores**

| *S. No.* | *Educational Qualification* | *No. of respondents* | *Mean Score* |
|---|---|---|---|
| 1. | School Level | 26 | 43.00 |
| 2. | Graduate | 221 | 46.31 |
| 3. | Post Graduate | 153 | 45.88 |

The highest mean score of adoption of coping strategies was found among graduate employees and the lowest among the school educated. The mean scores are found different among the three groups. The significance of the difference is tested by formulating the following null hypothesis.

*Null hypothesis:* There is no significant difference among bank employees belonging to different educational groups with respect to coping strategies (Each coping strategy is considered individually).

**Table 4.75**

**Summary of ANOVA 'F' Ratios for Coping Strategies with Respect to Educational Qualification**

| | 1 | 2 | 3 | 4 | 5 | 6 | 7 | 8 | 9 |
|---|---|---|---|---|---|---|---|---|---|
| *Coping strategies* | *Relaxation techniques* | *Strategies of preparations* | *Elicitation of social support* | *Distraction techniques* | *Rational task oriented behaviour* | *Passive attempts* | *Emotional relief* | *Instant reaction* | *Organisational strategies* |
| **F Ratios** | 1.1413 (NS) | 5.1211* | 14.16545* | 5.0251* | 7.2941* | 1.704 (NS) | 10.281* | 3.2518* | 1.1777 (NS) |

* Significant at 5% level.

NS— Not Significant.

Coping strategies one (Relaxation Techniques), six (Passive attempts) and nine (Organisational Strategies) are non-significant, and the rest of the strategies have emerged significant, being the reason for significant difference among employees with differing educational qualifications. Therefore, null hypothesis holds good for strategies one, six and nine and rejected for the rest of the strategies.

## Salary and Level of Adoption of Coping Strategies

The relation of salary drawn with the level of adoption of coping strategies is analysed here.

It is observed from Table 4.76 that high coping strategy group consists of higher percentage of those whose monthly salary is above Rs. 20,000

**Table 4.76**

**Salary and Level of Adoption of Coping Strategies**

| *S. No.* | *Salary* | *Level of adoption of coping strategies* | | | *Total* |
|---|---|---|---|---|---|
| | | *Low* | *Medium* | *High* | |
| 1. | Below Rs. 15000 | 22 (16.3) | 91 (67.4) | 22 (16.3) | 135 |
| 2. | Rs. 15000 - Rs. 20000 | 14 (12.5) | 78 (69.6) | 20 (17.9) | 112 |
| 3. | Above Rs.20000 | 4 (2.6) | 121 (79.1) | 28 (18.3) | 153 |
| | **Total** | **40** | **290** | **70** | **400** |

Table 4.77 shows the mean scores of adoption of coping strategies by the bank employees grouped into various categories according to their salary.

**Table 4.77**

**Salary and Level of Adoption of Coping Strategies – Mean Scores**

| *S. No.* | *Salary* | *No. of respondents* | *Mean score* |
|---|---|---|---|
| 1. | Below Rs.15000 | 135 | 44.51 |
| 2. | Rs.15000 – Rs.20000 | 112 | 45.43 |
| 3. | Above Rs.20000 | 153 | 47.55 |

Table 4.77 denotes higher mean score of adoption of coping strategies for those employees whose monthly salary is more than Rs.20000, followed by salary group of Rs. 15,000-Rs. 20,000 and below Rs. 15,000.

The significance of the difference is tested here.

*Null hypothesis:* There is no significant difference among employees earning different amounts of salary with respect to coping strategies (Each coping strategy is considered individually).

Table 4.78

**Summary of ANOVA 'F' Ratios for Coping Strategies with Respect to Salary**

| *Coping strategies* | 1 *Relaxation techniques* | 2 *Strategies of preparations* | 3 *Elicitation of social support* | 4 *Distraction techniques* | 5 *Rational task oriented behaviour* | 6 *Passive attempts* | 7 *Emotional relief* | 8 *Instant reaction* | 9 *Organisational strategies* |
|---|---|---|---|---|---|---|---|---|---|
| F Ratios | 4.9161* | 4.5027* | 3.4918* | 6.9241* | 6.9847* | 9.6669* | 3.2053* | 1.8947 (NS) | 0.8148 (NS) |

* Significant at 5% level.

NS— Not Significant.

Coping strategies, eight (Instant Reaction) and nine (Organisational Strategies) have emerged non-significant, whereas the rest of the coping strategies are significant, accounting for the significant difference among employees belonging to different income groups. Therefore, the null hypothesis is accepted for coping strategies eight and nine and rejected for the rest of the strategies.

## Type of Bank and Level of Adoption of Coping Strategies

Table 4.79 shows the level of adoption of coping strategies by the employees of public sector and private sector banks.

From Table 4.79 it is understood that higher percentage of employees both the types of banks adopted medium level of strategies. High level strategies were adopted by higher percentage of the employees of private sector banks than public sector banks.

Table 4.79

Type of Bank and Level of Adoption of Coping Strategies

| *S. No.* | *Type of Bank* | *Level of Adoption of Coping Strategies* | | | *Total* |
|---|---|---|---|---|---|
| | | *Low* | *Medium* | *High* | |
| 1. | Private | 22 (20.8) | 81 (76.4) | 3 (2.8) | 106 |
| 2. | Public | 43 (14.6) | 247 (84.0) | 4 (1.4) | 294 |
| | **Total** | **40** | **290** | **70** | **400** |

Table 4.80

Type of Bank and Level of Adoption of Coping Strategies – Mean Scores

| *S. No.* | *Type of Bank* | *No. of Respondents* | *Mean Score* |
|---|---|---|---|
| 1. | Private | 106 | 45.78 |
| 2. | Public | 294 | 44.45 |

Mean scores of adoption of coping strategies given in Table 4.80 also show higher mean scores for private sector bank employees.

The significance of the above difference is statistically tested here.

*Null hypothesis:* There is no significant difference between the bank employees belonging to public sector and private sector banks with respect to various coping strategies (Each coping strategy is considered individually).

In Table 4.81 Coping strategies four (Distraction Techniques), six (Passive Attempts), seven (Emotional Relief) and eight (Instant Reaction) are non-significant, and the remaining strategies have emerged significant, being the reason for significant difference among employees of the public sector and private sector banks. Therefore, the null hypothesis is accepted for strategies, four, six, seven and eight and rejected for rest of the strategies.

Table 4.81

Summary of ANOVA 'F' Ratios for Coping Strategies with Respect to Type of Bank

| Coping strategies | 1 Relaxation techniques | 2 Strategies of preparations | 3 Elicitation of social support | 4 Distraction techniques | 5 Rational task oriented behaviour | 6 Passive attempts | 7 Emotional relief | 8 Instant reaction | 9 Organisational strategies |
|---|---|---|---|---|---|---|---|---|---|
| F Ratios | 1.7646* | 10.5095* | 11.8519* | 0.0107 (NS) | 9.814* | 1.7486 (NS) | 2.6199 (NS) | 1.9097 (NS) | 14.3209* |

* Significant at 5% level.

NS— Not Significant.

**Nature of Job and Level of Adoption of Coping Strategies**

Here, an attempt has been made to study the dependence of level of adoption of coping strategies on the nature of job of employees. In this regard, ANOVA test has been conducted to analyse whether there is any significant relationship between nature of job and level of adoption of coping strategies.

Table 4.82 denotes high coping for higher percentage of the clerical staff. Level of coping is found different for the groups with different nature of job.

Table 4.83 portrays different mean scores for the four categories, the highest being 45.51 for those who are officers by nature of job.

Table 4.82

Nature of Job and Level of Adoption of Coping Strategies

| *S. No.* | *Nature of job* | *Level of adoption of coping strategies* | | | *Total* |
|---|---|---|---|---|---|
| | | *Low* | *Medium* | *High* | |
| 1. | Manager | 18 (3.9) | 105 (79.7) | 5 (16.4) | 128 |
| 2. | Assistant Manager | 7 (18.4) | 31 (57.9) | 0 (23.7) | 38 |
| 3. | Officer | 3 (3.2) | 59 (79.4) | 1 (17.4) | 63 |
| 4. | Clerk | 12 (7.0) | 95 (55.5) | 64 (37.5) | 171 |
| | **Total** | **40** | **290** | **70** | **400** |

Table 4.83

Nature of Job and Level of Adoption of Coping Strategies – Mean Scores

| *S. No.* | *Nature of job* | *No. of respondents* | *Mean score* |
|---|---|---|---|
| 1. | Manager | 128 | 45.41 |
| 2. | Assistant Manager | 38 | 44.68 |
| 3. | Officer | 63 | 45.51 |
| 4. | Clerk | 171 | 43.63 |

The significance of the difference is tested by framing the following null hypothesis.

*Null Hypothesis:* There is no significant difference among employees having different nature of jobs with respect to coping strategies (Each coping strategy is considered individually).

Coping strategies three (Elicitation of Social Support), four (Distraction Techniques), five (Rational Task Oriented Behaviour) and eight (Instant Reaction) have emerged significant, whereas the rest of the coping strategies are non-significant. Coping strategies, three, four, five and eight have accounted for significant difference among employees belonging to different nature of jobs. Therefore, the null hypothesis is rejected for coping strategies three, four, five and eight and accepted for the rest of the coping strategies.

**Table 4.84**

**Summary of ANOVA 'F' Ratios for Coping Strategies with Respect to Nature of Job**

| | 1 | 2 | 3 | 4 | 5 | 6 | 7 | 8 | 9 |
|---|---|---|---|---|---|---|---|---|---|
| *Coping strategies* | *Relaxation techniques* | *Strategies of preparations* | *Elicitation of social support* | *Distraction techniques* | *Rational task oriented behaviour* | *Passive attempts* | *Emotional relief* | *Instant reaction* | *Organisational strategies* |
| **F Ratios** | 0.4254 (NS) | 1.2387 (NS) | 5.2909* | 11.8447* | 8.522* (NS) | 0.1622 (NS) | 0.7168 | 5.2572* (NS) | 1.8154 |

* Significant at 5% level.

NS— Not Significant.

**Length of Service ar⁻ᵈ Level of Adoption of Coping Strategies**

Table 4.85 shows the level of adoption of coping strategies by bank employees of different periods of service.

It is evident from Table 4.85 that there is difference among the employees of different periods of service with respect to their stress coping.

Table 4.86 shows the mean scores of bank employees of different lengths of service regarding the adoption of coping strategies.

Table 4.85

**Length of Service and Level of Adoption of Coping Strategies**

| *S. No.* | *Length of service* | *Level of adoption of coping strategies* | | | *Total* |
|---|---|---|---|---|---|
| | | *Low* | *Medium* | *High* | |
| 1. | Below 5 years | 8 (7.6) | 72 (68.6) | 25 (23.8) | 105 |
| 2. | 6-10 years | 16 (9.0) | 141 (79.7) | 20 (11.3) | 177 |
| 3. | Above 10 years | 16 (13.5) | 77 (65.3) | 25 (21.2) | 118 |
| | **Total** | **40** | **290** | **70** | **400** |

Table 4.86

**Length of Service and Level of Adoption of Coping Strategies – Mean Scores**

| *S. No.* | *Length of service* | *No. of respondents* | *Mean score* |
|---|---|---|---|
| 1. | Below 5 years | 105 | 46.84 |
| 2. | 6-10 years | 177 | 45.37 |
| 3. | Above 10 years | 118 | 45.97 |

Mean scores as shown in Table 4.86 also reveal the difference according to the difference in periods of service.

The significance of the difference is tested for which the following null hypothesis is framed.

*Null Hypothesis:* There is no significant difference among employees having different periods of service with respect to coping strategies (Each coping strategy is considered individually).

In Table 4.87 Coping strategies, three (Elicitation of Social Support), four (Distraction Techniques) and six (Passive Attempts) have emerged significant, having accounted for the significance of the difference among the bank employees of different periods of service. The rest of the strategies have emerged non-significant. Therefore, the null hypothesis is rejected for coping strategies three, four and six and accepted for rest of the strategies.

**Table 4.87**

**Summary of ANOVA 'F' Ratios for Coping Strategies with Respect to Length of Service**

| | 1 | 2 | 3 | 4 | 5 | 6 | 7 | 8 | 9 |
|---|---|---|---|---|---|---|---|---|---|
| *Coping Strategies* | *Relaxation techniques* | *Strategies of preparations* | *Elicitation of social support* | *Distraction techniques* | *Rational task oriented behaviour* | *Passive attempts* | *Emotional relief* | *Instant reaction* | *Organisational strategies* |
| **F Ratios** | 0.1176 (NS) | 0.1697 (NS) | 5.8953* | 3.612* | 0.6368 (NS) | 3.9786* | 0.2249 (NS) | 0.6378 (NS) | 2.9008 (NS) |

* Significant at 5% level.

NS— Not Significant.

## CONCLUSION

The results of the analysis done in this chapter with respect to the level of occupational stress and influencing factors indicate that:

Majority of the sampled employees (63 per cent) experienced medium level of stress. Twenty one percentage had experienced high stress while stress level was low among sixteen percentage of the respondents. Among those categorised on the basis of demographic and job related factors, employees below 35 years, female employees, unmarried category, post-graduates by education, public sector bank employees, clerical staff and employees with shorter period of service were the groups with high levels of job stress.

From the analysis done with respect to sources of job stress it was found that organisational factors such as role factors and job factors, extra-organisational factors, group factors and individual factors were the major stressors.

Demographic variables such as age and educational qualification had significant influence over the stressors.

From the analysis of the relationship between personality type and stress management ability it is concluded that the degree of correlation between personality type *A* and the stress management ability is low in the case of both managerial and non-managerial cadres. Personality type *B* as well as *AB* exhibited high degree of correlation with stress resistance for managerial personnel and low degree of correlation in the case of non-managerial category.

It is clear from the analysis done with respect to the effect of job stress that bank employees experience fatigue and quantity of work in banks gets affected due to job stress. However, stressful situations have not created the intention to quit among the employees and their job involvement has not been affected.

As regards coping strategies, 'Instant Reaction', 'Rational Task Oriented Behaviour', 'Emotional Relief' and 'Passive Attempts' emerged as the significant coping strategies. Comparisons of means indicate that significant differences exist between respondents belonging to different age groups, gender, education, salary, type of bank, nature of job and length of service with respect to adoption of coping strategies.

# Chapter–5

# SUMMARY OF FINDINGS, SUGGESTIONS AND CONCLUSION

## INTRODUCTION

Globalisation and Information Technology are currently transforming the Indian banking radically. Advances in technology have become the most important factor for dealing with the intensifying competition and rapid proliferaticn of financial innovations. Survival of the fittest has become the order of the day. In order to be most fit, an organisation has to achieve perfection with respect to all factors of production, especially with human factor. The employees of any organisation have to be kept fully satisfied and happy so that productivity, efficiency and performance will be at its peak. The employees can be happy only if job stress is avoided.

Stress is inevitable for most people in most jobs today. Stress can be understood as a condition of strain on one's emotions, thoughts, processes and physical conditions. It affects personality, perceptions, feelings, attitudes and behaviour of the human beings. When they are continuously exposed to stress, psychological or physical damage results. On the other hand, when there is no stress, job challenges are absent and performance tends to be low. As stress increases upto a particular level, performance tends to increase, because stress helps a person to meet the job requirements. It is a healthy stimulus that encourages employees to respond to challenges. But if stress increases beyond a particular level, performance begins to decline.

People have different tolerance levels when they face a stressful situation. Some people are easily upset by the slightest change or emergency. Others are cool, calm and well composed because they have confidence in their ability to cope with stressful situations. All these are dependent on one's personality type. In relation to different personality characteristics, another element of stress related outcomes is the way an individual copes and manages stress.

Studies on stress would help individuals and organisations evolve effective coping strategies. Very few studies have taken into consideration the various aspects of stress such as employees' stress level, sources of stress, effects of stress and coping strategies. Hence, this study entitled 'Occupational Stress of Bank Employees – A Study in Erode District, Tamil Nadu' has been undertaken by the researcher to make an in-depth analysis of the above stated aspects of occupational stress.

This study is based on survey method. Primary data were collected through a structured questionnaire. Suitable statistical tools were employed in the analysis of data.

## FINDINGS

The main findings of the study detailed in Chapter IV are summarised and given as follows:

### Level of Occupational Stress and Influencing Factors

It is observed from the analysis that bank employees were experiencing stress and the stress levels identified were medium for higher percentage (63) of the respondents, 21 per cent experiencing high and 16 per cent low levels of stress.

Analysis of the influence of demographic variables and job related variables on the levels of job stress indicated that, among the different age groups, higher percentage of the employees below 35 years are more prone to high job stress. Young employees (below 35 years of age) have more stress than the middle aged and old aged employees. It may be explained here that older employees may have more maturity in their outlook and approach. They are more familiar with work environment and other work related problems. The difference between the level of stress as indicated by the stress scores between the young and old may be attributed to the above stated reasons.

As regards gender groups are concerned, female employees constitute higher percentage of the high level stress group. Analysis based on marital status revealed that unmarried employees' stress level were higher than that of the married.

Employees with higher qualification (post-graduates) constitute higher percentage of the employees with high level of stress. Employees drawings lower amounts of salary are prone to high level of stress. This may be due to the feeling of inequity when compared to employees drawing higher salary.

Comparison of public sector and private sector bank employees revealed marginal difference in the mean stress score, that of public sector bank slightly higher.

Stress scores of the clerical staff were found higher when compared to the other categories of bank employees. Longer the service lower is the job stress of employees.

It is observed from the results of chi-square test that there is significant difference in the stress level of bank employees according to factors such as age, gender, marital status, education, salary drawn, and nature of job. However there are no significant differences in the level of stress of employees categorised on the basis of types of banks such as public sector and private sector bank employees and among employees differing in their length of service.

### Sources of Job Stress

It is observed from the results of factor analysis that the significant causes of job stress which have been identified in the order of importance are 'Role ambiguity, Role conflict and Absence of role authority', 'Role overload and Lack of leadership support', Role stagnation and mismatch', Role anxiety and 'Feeling of inequity', 'Feeling of being paid low', 'Extra organisational factors', 'Lack of interpersonal relationship', 'Personality traits', 'Difficulty in performing the job' and 'Lack of group cohesiveness and Role description'.

With respect to 'Role ambiguity' the main reason as to why employees experience stress is because responsibilities are more general in nature and the task specifications are not clear.

Absence of 'Role authority' arises when authority is not commensurate with responsibility and authority is dispersed and gets diluted at various levels of hierarchy which has been a cause of stress for the employees.

Employees experience 'Role overload' because of the time deadlines with respect to the bank transactions. This is a foremost reason for the presence of role overload because working under extreme time pressure is stressful and employees adjustment to work gets distracted resulting in negative attitude towards the job.

As regards 'Lack of leadership support' inconsiderate behaviour of superiors make the employees feel letdown and irritated resulting in job stress.

The stressor 'Role stagnation' can be related to fewer opportunities for learning and growth for the bank employees.

Bank employees feeling that they get less salary compared to the quantity and responsibilities in their work has developed a 'Feeling of inequity' and negative attitude towards their job resulting in stress.

'Lack of Group cohesiveness' is experienced by employees because employees are interrelated by a network of personal relationship. So the pattern of relationship influence the group and their attitude towards their job. Because of the intra group conflicts negative attitudes have developed. Thus lack of group cohesiveness emerged as a significant stressor.

**Demographic Variables and Stressors**

As regards the demographic variables all the stressors i.e., individual factors, group factors, organisational-role factors, organisational-job factors and extra organisational factors have emerged significant at 95 per cent confidence level. The difference among the age groups is attributed to the difference in level of maturity of the employees on account of job and life experience.

With respect to gender all the stressors are non-significant indicating no difference between male and female employees as regards sources of stress.

With respect to education it is noted that all the stressors cause significant difference among the three educational categories. Of all the stressors individual factors emerged most significant, the reason may be attributed to the difference in the skills exhibited by the employees which differ according to their educational qualification.

When analysis of variance was done considering income, only Group factors and Role factors have emerged significant and the remaining three factors were not significant. This proves that employees belonging to different income groups are not significantly different from each other with majority of the stressors.

As regards the type of bank, results of analysis of variance indicate that none of the stressors cause significant difference among the employees of public sector and private sector banks.

On the basis of designation, the findings reveal that, of the five stressors, only two, such as Role and Job factors are significant. It can be inferred from this that the responsibilities to be performed and accountability differ according to nature of job causing significant difference regarding role and job factors.

ANOVA results on the basis of length of service reveal that all the stressors are not significant. Familiarity with work environment, good relationship build with superiors and subordinates irrespective of length of service are the contributing factors causing no differences among employees with varying years of service.

**Discriminant Analysis Between High Stress and Low Stress Group**

It has been found from the results of discriminant function analysis that totally 13 variables discriminate between high and low stress group. Of these, 'Extra-organisational factors', 'Organisational-job factors', 'Organisational-role factors', and 'Group factors' cause major differences between the high and low stress groups of employees.

**Personality Type and Stress Management Ability**

Personality type of majority of the sampled bank employees is 'Personality type *AB*' in both the managerial (94.58 per cent) and non-managerial (94.88 per cent) cadres.

Higher percentage of the employees belonging to both managerial (54.22 per cent) and non-managerial (64.10 per cent) categories are found to have fair stress management ability.

Correlation analysis conducted to test the relationship between Personality type *A*, and stress management ability revealed low degree of correlation in case of both the managerial and non-managerial categories.

As regard Personality type *B* and stress management ability of managerial personnel, the degree of correlation is positive and high. In case of non-managerial category, the correlation co-efficient is positive but negligible. It implies that the stress management ability of managerial Personnel in type *B* category is significantly related with the Personality type. High politeness, less competitive and non-aggressive characters contribute to high stress management ability.

The analysis further revealed a high degree of positive correlation between Personality type *AB* and stress management ability in the case of managerial cadre and low degree of correlation in the case of non-managerial personnel. So it may be concluded that a combination of the characteristics of Personality type *A* and Personality type *B* influences the way, the bank employees of the managerial category manage their stress.

### Effects of Job Stress

Weighted average scores have been computed to study the effects of job stress on the individuals and the organisation.

The weighted scores indicate that job stress have a stimulating effects on individuals, that they have no intention to quit their job and also they exhibited more job involvement. However, fatigue, tension and job dissatisfaction are some the negative effects of job stress on individuals, but the positive effects outweighed these negative effects.

As regards effects on the organisation, negative impact has been noted on quantity of work followed by quality of work. The least effect was found on absenteeism.

### Coping Strategies

Factor analysis has been used to identify the effective coping strategies followed by the bank employees. The coping strategies which have been adopted by the bank employees in their order of importance are 'Rational Task oriented behaviour' and 'Instant Reactions', 'Relief Techniques', 'Organisational Strategies', 'Strategies of Preparation', 'Distraction Techniques', 'Impressive Approach', 'Eliciting Social Support' and 'Passive Attempts'.

'Rational task oriented behaviour' is a work-focussed strategy. Employees can decrease stress by directly changing their own work habits and setting priorities to their job.

Relief techniques like yoga, meditation and forms of physical exercises indicate the adoption of a healthy way of coping with stress by the sampled employees. It is an emotion focussed strategy which does not have a direct impact on work environment, but rather helps employees adjust to stress more easily.

The 'Organisational strategies' show that banks conduct stress reduction workshops, leadership training programmes and health maintenance programmes in which employees are participating.

Strategies of preparation to face stressful work situation like taking a day off in order to feel fresh appears to be a very effective coping strategy adopted by the bank employees.

Forgetting the problem is adopted as a distraction technique by the present sample to cope up job stress.

Eliciting social support like discussing work related problems with friends and family members and passive attempts like ignoring the problem and expecting superiors support are also effective coping strategies adopted by the sample.

From the weighted average analysis done to determine the most commonly adopted strategies in an order, 'Instant reaction', 'Rational task oriented behaviour' and 'Emotional relief' emerged as the first three among the coping methods adopted by the sample and 'Distraction techniques' emerged as the least adopted coping method.

**Coping Strategies and Demographic Variables**

Comparisons made among different age groups revealed that coping strategies adoption differ among the age groups with maximum difference for 'Elicitation of social support' followed by 'Relaxation techniques' and 'Emotional relief'. There are no significant differences in the adoption of other coping strategies by the three age groups. Level of adoption of coping strategies was found to be low among the middle aged category (36 years-50 years).

Significant difference between the gender groups is found only with regard to the adoption, of 'Organisational strategies' and 'Distraction techniques'. Level of adoption of coping strategies was found lower in the case of female employees.

With respect to education, it is found that there exists no difference among the three educational categories as regards the adoption of 'Relaxation techniques', 'Passive attempts' and 'Organisational strategies'. Level of adoption of other strategies is different among these groups. Elicitation of social support is the coping method showing the maximum difference among the groups, school level category is found to have adopted the lowest level of adoption of the coping strategies.

Taking into account the type of bank, the maximum difference is found in the adoption of 'Organisational coping strategies' by the public sector and private sector bank employees. Private sector bank employees coping strategies adoption score is found to be high.

A comparison of different designation categories revealed significant differences in the adoption of 'Distraction techniques', 'Rational task oriented behaviour', 'Elicitation of social support' and 'Instant reaction'. Higher percentage of the clerical cadre has adopted high level of coping.

Taking into account the length of service, adoption of coping strategies, like 'Elicitation of social support', 'Passive attempts' and 'Distraction techniques' are causing differences among the employees, while adoption of other strategies do not differ among these categories.

On the basis of salary, 'Instant reaction' and 'Organisational strategies' do not cause any difference among employees. Whereas, the adoption of all the other strategies differ according to difference in the salary of the employees. Among the three categories, those drawing higher salary has adopted more coping methods.

## SUGGESTIONS

The findings of the study show Role ambiguity, Role conflict, Role overload, Role stagnation and mismatch, Lack of leadership support, Role anxiety, Difficulty in performing the job, Lack of interpersonal relationship and Lack of group cohesiveness as the sources of stress. Hence the following suggestions are made here.

### Job Analysis and Job Clarification

Job analysis and clarification is necessary to deal with job ambiguity and job conflict involving both the employees and the superiors through effective discussions.

### Working Collaboratively

To deal with role overload, an open work environment should be created which would allow employees to work collaboratively, thereby reducing job stress.

### Job Redesign

Role stagnation is found to be a stressor for the employees which can be reduced by job enrichment involving redefining and restructuring a job and making it more meaningful and challenging.

### Training Programmes

Mismatch between employees capability and the requirements of job as a sources of job stress can be reduced by arranging training programmes by the bank focussing on knowledge acquisition and skill development for the employees.

### Knowledge Updating Programmes

Role anxiety of the employees caused by changes in technological upgradations shall be reduced through knowledge updating programmes which will help employees to face challenges brought up by technological environment.

### Time Management

Difficulty in performing the job within the stipulated time has been identified as a stressor. Hence employees may be instructed to keep a log of the time they spent on specific duties for a period. Analysis of this logs can help employees to determine the factual allocation of time which matches the duties and responsibilities of the job.

### Equitable Distribution of Work Load

Work overload should be reduced by equitable distribution of the work so that work can be easily handled by the employees.

### Developing Harmonious Relationship Between Superiors and Subordinates

Stress caused by lack of inter-personal relationship can be reduced if a harmonious relationship is developed between superiors and subordinates.

### Feedback Mechanism

A highly developed systematic, frequent and accurate feedback mechanism should be implemented in banks so that the attitude and feelings of the employees regarding their jobs is known. Accordingly motivation programmes can be developed by the bank.

**Formulating a Rational New Entry Programme**

Banks should formulate a new entry programme involving several rotational assignments, training sessions and also assigning the new recruits to a supportive mentor to offer support to reduce the job anxiety of the employees.

**Employee Counselling**

Employees at the lower cadre are found to have stress because of their feeling inequity. Counselling helps the organisation to be more considerate towards employees problems. Employees may also develop self confidence and understanding to work effectively.

**Relocation Bonus**

Stress arising from extra organisational sources such as problems of relocation of family can be reduced if the employees are paid relocation bonus as per their needs.

As regards coping strategies and mitigating the negative effects of the job stress the following suggestions are offered.

**Making Organisational Strategies More Effective**

It is found from the analysis that the level of adoption of coping strategies by women employees are less when compared to men especially the organisational coping strategies. Hence women employees should be encouraged to participate in stress reduction workshops and health maintenance programmes organised by the bank. Stress management programmes should be designed to teach the employees healthy coping strategies which reduce work related problems.

**Prioritising Duties**

Job stress is found to have affected the quantity of work done by the employees. Hence prioritisation of work, goal setting and identification of work will enable employees to accomplish the required task.

**Developing Positive Attitude**

Employees who are more flexible, relaxed and positive are found to have better stress resistance than those who are rigid and with negative attitude. Hence employees should develop a positive attitude towards work and work related environment.

**Practicing Yoga and Meditation**

'Fatigue' and 'Tension' are found to be some of the effects of job stress on the employees. Hence employees are required to practice yoga and meditation regularly to keep them physically fit and make their mind relaxed and calm.

## CONCLUSION

From this study it is concluded that Bank employees are experiencing job stress and are varying based on the differences in their demographic variables. Important causes of job stress among bank employees are Role ambiguity, Role conflicts, Absence of role authority, Lack of leadership support, Role stagnation, Lack of group cohesiveness and Extra organisational factors.

Job stress has resulted in both positive and negative effects on individuals and banks, positive effects outweighed negative effects.

Coping strategies such as Rational Task oriented behaviour, Instant reactions, Relief techniques, Organisational strategies, Strategies of preparation, Distraction techniques, Impressive approach, Eliciting social support and passive attempts are adopted by the bank employees.

## SCOPE FOR FURTHER RESEARCH

The researcher is pleased to offer the following areas for further research by future researchers undertaking research in occupational stress.

1. Occupational stress of IT professionals.
2. Effective coping strategies for the employees of multinationals to bridge the family-work place gap.

# BIBLIOGRAPHY

**BOOKS**

Aiken, L.R., (1982); *Psychological Testing and Assessment.* Boston: Allyan and Bacon, inc.

Allen, Louis A., *Management and Organisation*, New York, McGraw-Hill Book Co., Inc., 1958.

Altrocci, J., Palmer, J., Hellman, R., and Davis, H (1968): The Marlowe - Growne, Repressor – Sensitizer, and Internal-External Scales and Attribution of Unconscious Hostile Intent. *Psychological Reports*, 23, 1229-1230.

Anastasi, A. (1982); *Psychological Testing*, Macmillan Publishing Co., Inc., New York.

Argyris, C. (1964); *Integrating the Individual and the Organisation.* New York: Wiley.

Basil, Douglas S. (1971); *Leadership Skills for Executive Action*, New York, American Management Association.

Beach, Dale S. (1980); *Personnel: The Management of People at Work*, New York, MacMillan.

Benson, Herbert, (1977); *The Relaxation Response*, Found, London.

Biddle, B.J., & Thomas, E.J., (1966); *Role Theory: Concepts and Research*. New York. Willey.

Branden, Nathaniel, (1969); *The Psychology of Self-esteem*, Bantam Books, Los Angels.

Caplan, R.D., Cobb, S., French, J.R.P., Jr., Harrison, R.V., & Pinneau s.r., Jr. (1975); *Job Demands and Worker Health: Main Effects and Occupational Differences*. Wahsington, D.C.: US. Government Printing Office.

Chhabra, T.N., Ahuja, K.K., and Jain, S.P. (1977); *Managing People at Work*, Delhi, Danpat Rai & Sons,.

Chhabra T.N. and Taneja P.L. (2005); *Essentials of Organisational Behaviour*, Dhanpat Rai & Co., Delhi.

Cherniss, C., (1980a); *Staff Burnout: Job Stress in the Human Services*. Beverly Hills, CA: Sage.

Davis, Keith, (1998); Human Behaviour at Work, *Organisational Behaviour*, New York, McGraw-Hill Book Co.,.

Edwards, A.L., (1959); Edwards Personal Preference Schedule, *The Psychological Corporation*, New York.

Edwards, A.L., (1957); *The Social Desirability Variable in Personality Assessment and Research*. New York, Dryden.

Faunce, W., (1968); *Social Problems of an Industrial Civilisation*, New York, McGraw Hill.

Fred Luthans, (1995); *Organisational Behaviour*, McGraw-Hill, Inc., New York, International Editions.

Fisher, R.A., (1950); *Statistical Methods for Research Workers*, New York Hafner Publishing Co.

Freudenberger, H.J., & Richelson, G., (1980); *Burnout: The High Cost and High Achievement*. New York: Anchor Press.

Friedman, M., & Rosenman, R.H., (1974); *Type A Behaviour an Dyour Heart*. New York: Alfred A. Knopf.

Garrett (1985); *Statistics in Psychology and Education*, Vakils, Feffer and Simons Private Ltd., Bombay.

Glasser, W., (1976); *Positive Addiction.* New York; Harper and Row.

Greg Vance, *Live a Better Life – How to Think and Achieve Success*, Master Mind Books, Bangalore.

Guilford, J.P., (1956); *Personality*, New York: McGraw – Hill.

Gupta M.K., (2002); *How to Control Mind and Be Stress-free*, Pustak Mahal, New Delhi, 10th Edition.

Herzberg, F., Mausner, B & Synderman, B.B. (1959); *The Motivation to Work.* John Wiley & Sons, Inc. New York.

Iyer (1971); *Purananooru Moolamum Pazaya Uraium* (in Tamil). Madras: V.V. Swaminatha Iyer Library.

Jacques, E., (1970); *Work, Creativity and Social Justice.* New York, International University Press.

Jacques, M., (1982); *Employment and Unemployment: A Social-Psychological Analysis.* Cambridge: Cambridge University Press.

Joshi Vinay, *Stress from Burnout to Balance*, Response Books, New Delhi, 2005.

Kahn, R.L., Wolfe, D.M., Quinn, Snook, J.D & Rosenthal R.A (1964); *Organisational Stress: Studies in Role Conflict an Ambiguity.* New York: Wiley.

Korman, A.K (1977); *Organisational Behaviour.* New Jersey, Prentice-Hall.

Kornhause, A (1965); *Mental Health of the Industrial Worker*, New York Willy.

Lachman, V.D., (1983); *Stress Management: A Manual for Nurse*, Grune & Stration, Inc., New York.

Lazarus, R.S., & Launier, R., (1978); *Stress-related Transactions Between Person and Environment.* In L.A. Pervin & M. Lewis (Eds.). *Internal and External Determinants of Behaviour.* New York; Plenum.

Likert, R (1961); *New Patterns of Management.* New York: McGraw—Hill.

Lindgran, H.C., (1973); *An Introduction to Social Psychology*. Wiley Eastern Pvt. Ltd., New Delhi.

Litwin & Stringer (1968); *Motivation and Organisational Climate*. Cambridge, Mass: Harward University Press.

Luthans, F (1981); *Organisational Behaviour*. McGraw-Hill International Book Company.

Maier, N.R.F., (1976); *Psychology in Industry*. Oxford & IBH Publishing Co., New Delhi.

Malcom, J., (1980); *The Impossible Profession* (Part I). New York, 55-133.

March, J.G., & Simon, H.A., (1958); Organisations. New York; Wiley.

Marx. K., (1973); *Selected Writings in Sociology and Social Philosophy* (Ed.). Bottomore, T.B., & Rubel. M., Middesex. Penquin Books.

Maslach, C., & Pines, A., (1979); *Burnout: The Loss of Human Caring*. In A. Pines & C. Maslach (Eds.), *Experiencing Social Psychology*. New York: Knopf.

Maslow, A.H. (1962); *Toward a Psychology of Being*, Princetion, Van Nostrand.

McGrath, J.E., (Ed.) (1970); *Social and Psychological Factors in Stress*. New York: Holt, Rinehart & Winston.

McGrath, J.E., (1976); *Stress and Behaviour in Organisations*. In Dunnette, M.D (Ed). *Handbook of Industrial and Organisational Psychology,* Rand Mcnally College Publishing Company, Chicago.

Merton, R.K (1957); *Social Theory and Social Structure*. Glencoe, Ill: The Free Press.

Millham, J., & Jacobson, L.I (1978); *The Need for Approval*, In London H., & Exner, J.E., Dimension of Personality (Ed)., New York, John Wiley & Sons.

Moorhead Gregory and Griffin Ricky W, *Organisational Behaviour*, Houghton Mifflin Company, Boston, 2nd Edition, 1989.

Moreno, J.L. (1934); *Who Shall Survive*? Washington, D.C., Nervous and Mental Diseases Publishing Co.

Nanda Meena, *A Handbook on Stress Management*, Indialog Publications Pvt. Ltd., New Delhi, 2006.

Newcomb, T.M., (1950); *Social Psychology*, NY: Dryden.

Orlick, T.D., and Botterill, C., (1975); *Every Kid Can Win*. Nelson-Hall Chicago.

Paine, W.S., (1981); *Burnout in Context*. In J.W. Jones(Ed.), *The Burnout Syndrome*. Park Ridge, IL: London House Management Press.

Paine, W.S., (Ed.), (1982); *Job Stress and Burnout Research, Theory and Intervention Perspectives*. Sage Publications, New Delhi.

Parsons, T., (1952); *The Social System*, Glenco, Free Press.

Payne, R.L., (1971); *Organisational Climate: The Concept and Research Findings*., Prakseologia.

Pines, A., (1982a); *Helpers' Motivation and the Burnout Syndrome*. In T.A. WILLS (Ed.), *Basic Processes in Helping Relationships,* New York: Academic Press.

Pines, A., (1982b); *On Burnout and the Buffering Effects of Social Support*. In B.Farber (Ed.), *Stress and Burnout in Human Service Professions*. New York: Pergamon.

Pines, A., (1982c); *Changing Organisations: Is a Work Environment Without Burnout an Impossible Goal* ? in. W.S Paine (Ed.), Job Stress and Burnout, Research, Theory and Intervention Perspectives. Sage, New Delhi.

Pines, A., & Aronson, E., (1980b); *A Self Diagnosis Instrument*. University of California, Berkeley.

Pines, A., & Aronson, E., & Kafry, D., (1981); *Burnout: From Tedium to Personal Growth*. New York: Free Press.

Quinn, R., & Shepard, L., (1974); *The 1972-73 Quality of Employment Survey*. Ann Arbor: University Of Michigan, Survey Research Center.

Rorschach, H., (1921); *Psychodiagnostics*, Hans Huber, Medical Publisher, Bern, Switzerland.

Rotter, J.B., Chance, J.E and Phares, E.J., (1972); *Applications of the Social Learning Theory of Personality*, Hoet, Rinehart and Winston, New York.

Sarason, S.B., (1977); *Work, Aging, and Social Change*. New York: Free Press.

Sarbin, T.R., & Allen, V.L., (1954); *Role Theory*. In Lindzey. G., & Aronson, E., (Ed.): The Handbook of Social Psychology. Vol.1. Addition-Leasley.

Saribin T.R., and Turner, R.H., (1972); *Role: Psychological and Sociological Aspects*. In Gill, D.L.L., International Encylopaedia of Social Science. Mac Millans.

Schacht, R., (1971); *Alienation*, London, Geroge, Allen & Nwin.

Schiamberg, L. B & Smith, K.U., (1982); *Human Development*, Macmillan Publishing Co., Inc., New York.

Schweb, R.L., (1983); *Teachers Burnout: Beyond Psychobabble*. Theory in to Practice, 21, 27-33.

Schvab, R.L., & Iwanicki, E.F., (1982); *Perceived Role Conflict, Role Ambiguity Teacher Burnout*. Educational Administration Quarterly, 18.

Secord, P.F., & Backman, C.W., (1964); *Social Psychology*, NY: Mc Graw Hill.

Seidenderg, B & Snadowsky, A., (1976); *Social Psychology: An Introduction*, The Free Press, London.

Slligman, M.E.P., (1975); *Helplessness*. San Francisco: W.H. Freeman.

Sharma Umesh; *Stress Management Through Ancient Wisdom and Modern Science*, Excel Books, New Delhi, 1st Edition, 2005.

Shinn, M., (1982); *Methodological Issues: Evaluating and Using Information*. In W.S.Paine (Ed.), *Job Stress and Burnout*, Sage Publications, New Delhi.

Singh, H.G., (1980); *Personality Typology of Yoga: The Vedic Path.*

Singh, R.P., (1986); *Perceived Organisational Role Stress as Related to Mental Health Problems.* In Malik, A.K., (Ed.): *Personality Evaluation: Development of a Multiphase Measure.* Jainsons Publications, New Delhi.

Smith, R.E., (1980); *Development of an Integrated Coping Response Through Cognitive Affective Stress Management Training.* In I.G. Sarason & C.D. Spielberger (Eds.), *Stress and Anxiety,* Washington, DC: Hemisphere.

Steers, R.M., & Mowday, R.T., (1981); *Employee Turnover and Post Decision Accommodation Processes.* In I.L. Cummingsd & B.M. Staw (Eds.), *Research in Organisational Behaviour,* Greenwich, CT: JAI Press.

Subramaniam, S.K., *Stress (Causes, Prevention & Cure),* Abhishek Publications, Chandigarh, 2002.

Sutton Jan, *Thrive on Stress,* Better Yourself Books, Mumbai, 2000.

Tannembaum (1966); *Social Psychology of the Work Organisation.* Belmont: Wadsworth Publishing Co.Inc.

Udai Pareek (1988); *Organisational Behaviour Processes,* Rewat Publications, Jaipur.

Venings, R.L., & Spradley, J.P., (1981); *The Work Stress Connection: How to Cope with Job Burnout.* Boston: Little, Brown and Company.

Wanous, J.P (1980); *Organisational Entry: Recruitment, Selection and Socialisation of Newcomers,* Reading, MA: Addison – Wesley.

Wilder, J.E & Plutchik, R., (1982); *Preparing the Professional: Building Prevention into Training.* In W.S. Paine (Ed.), *Job Stress and Burnout: Research, Theory and Intervention Perspectives.* Beverly Hills: Sage Publications.

**JOURNALS/MAGAZINES**

Aiken, M & Hage (1966); Organisational Alienation—A Comparative Analysis. *American Sociological Review*, 31, 497-507.

Anderson, C.R (1976); Coping Behaviours as Intervening Mechanisms in the Inverted U Stress Performance Relationship. *Journal of Applied Psychology*, 61, 30-34.

Banikiotes, P.G., Russell, J.M., & Linden, J.D., (1971); Social Desirability, Adjustment and Effectiveness. *Psychological Reports*, 29, 581-582.

Barthel, C.E & Crowne, D.P (1962). The Need for Approval, Task Categorisation and Perceptual Defence. *Journal of Consulting Psychology*, 26, 547-555.

Bartolome, F., (1972). Executives as Human Beings. *Harward Business Review*, 50, 62-69.

Beehr, T.A., & Newman, J.E., (1978); Job Stress, Employee Health and Organisational Effectiveness: A Fact Analysis, Model and Literature Review, *Personal Psychology*, 31, 665-699.

Beehr, T.A., Walsh, J.T., & Taber T.D., (1976); Relationship of Stress to Individually and Organisationally Valued States: Higher Order Needs as a Moderator. *Journal of Applied Psychology*, 61, 14-47.

Birmingham, J.A., (1985); Job Satisfaction and Burnout Among Minesta Teachers. *Dissertation Abstracts International*, Vol. 45, No. 11, p. 3286A.

Blanks, C.D., (1985); The Determinants of Nursing Faculty Burnout. *Dissertation Abstracts International*, Vol. 45, No. 11 p. 3286A.

Brief, A.R., & Aldag, R.J., (1976); Correlates of the Role Indices. *Journal of Applied Psychology*, 61, 468-472.

Burke, R.J. (1976); Occupational Stresses and Job Satisfaction. *Journal of Social Psychology*, 100, 235-244.

Burke, R.J., & Becourt, M.L., (1974); Managerial Role Stress and Coping Responses. *Journal of Business Administration*, 5, 55-68.

Burke, A.J., & Deszca, E., (1986); Correlates of Psychological Burnout Phases Among Police Officers. *Human Relations*, Vol. 39, No. 6, 487-502.

Burke, R.J., Searer, J., & Deszca, G., (1984); Burnout Among Men and Women in Police Work: An Examination of the Cherniss Model. *Jhhra Fall*, 162-188.

Caccesse, T., & Mayerberg, C., (1984); Gender Difference in Perceived Burnout of College Coaches. *Journal of Sport Psychology*, 6, 279-288.

Chirayath Susan, (2006); A Study of the Relationship Between Personality and Stress Resistance/Management Ability in Employees, *The Icfaian Journal of Management Research*, May 2006, pp. 7-22.

Cobb, S., (1976); Social Support as Moderator of Life Stress. *Psychomatic Medicine*, 38, 300-314.

Constable, J.f., & Russell, D., (1986); The Effect of Social Support and the Work Environment Upon Burnout Among Nurses. *Journal of Human Stress*. 12, 20-26.

Cooper, C.L., & Marshall, J., (1976); Occupational Sources of Stress: A Review of the Literature Relating to Coronary Heart Disease and Mental Ill health. *Journal of Occupational Psychology*, 49, 11-28.

Corwin, R., (1961); The Professional Employee: A Study of Conflict Nursing Roles. *American Journal of Sociology*, 66, 604-615.

Crowne, D.P., & Marlowe, D., (1960); A Scale of Social Desirability Independent of Psychopathology. *Journal of Consulting Psychology*, 24, 349-354.

Farbar. B.A., & Heifetz, L.H., (1981); The Satisfaction and Stresses of Psychotherapeutic Work: A Factor Analytic Study. *Professional Psychology* 12 (5), 52-62.

Fishman, C.G., (1965); Need for Approval and the Expression of Aggression Under Varying Conditions of Frustration. *Journal of Personality and Social Psychology*, 214, 301-308.

Form, W.H., (1973); Aut. Workers and Their Machines: A Study of Work, Factory and Job Satisfaction in Four Countries. *Social Forces*, 52, 1-15.

Freebarin, H.A. (1984); The Pastor Unbound: An Exercise in Liberation and Nurturance. *Dissertation Abstracts International*. Vol. 45, No. 5, p. 1426A.

French, J.R.P., Jr., & Caplan, R.D., (1973); Organisational Stress and Individual Strain. In Marlow. A (Ed): The Failure of Success New York, *American Management Association*, 30-65.

Freudenberger, H.J., (1974); Staff Burnout. *Journal of Social Issues*, 30(1), 159-165.

Freudenberger, H.J., (1975); The Staff Burnout Syndrome in Alternative Institutions. *Psycholotherapy: Theory, Research and Practice*, 12(1), 73-88.

Freudenberger, H.J., (1977): Burnout; The Occupational Hazard of the Child Care Worker. *Child Care Quarterly*, Vol. 6, No. 2, 90-99.

Freudenberger, H.J., (1980): How to Survive Burnout. *Nation's Business*, 53-58.

Freudenberger, H.J., (1986) Impaired Clincians: Coping with Burnout. *In Innovations in Clinical Practice: A Source Book*. Vol. 3. Personal Communication.

Gaines, J., Jermier, J.M., (1983); Emotional Exhaustion in a High Stress Organisation. *Academy of Management Journal*, 26, 567-586.

Gani A, Farooq A. Shah, (1999); Job Stress Among Banking Employees: An Empirical Study, *Paradigm*, Vol. 2, No. 2, January 1999, pp. 21-39.

Gieck, J., Brown, R.S., & Shank, R.H., (1982); The Burnout Syndrome Among Athletic Trainers. *Athletic Training*, August, 36-41.

Goode, W.J. (1960); A Theory of Role Strain. *American Sociological Review*, 25, 483-496.

Gorden, L.V., (1967); *Survey of Personal Inventory*, Science Research Associates.

Guptha, N., & Beehr., T.A., (1979); Job Stress and Employees' Behaviour. *Organisational Behaviour and Human Performance*. 23, 373-387.

Hamner, W.C., & Tosi, H. (1974); Relationship of Role Conflict and Role Ambiguity to Job Involvement Measures. *Journal of Applied Psychology*, 59, 497-499.

Harigopal, K., (1980); Role Stress Variables and Company Satisfaction and Job Involvement: Personality Factors as Moderators. *Managerial Psychology*, 1, Vol. 2, 13-25.

Harmon-Vaught, D.S., (1986): Role Ambiguity, Personal and Professional Variables and Burnout Among Special Education Teachers. *Dissertation Abstracts International*. Vol. 47, No. 3, P. 862A.

Hollen, C.J., & Chesser, R.J., (1976); The Relationship of Personal Influence Dissonance to Job Tension, Satisfaction and Involvement. *Academy Management Journal*, Vol. 19, No. 2.

Horowitz, I.L., (1966); Alienation and the Social Order. *Philosophy and Phenomeno-Logical Research*, 27, 230-237.

Horst, W.C., (1986); The Relationships Among Adaptation, Stressors, Job Stress and Burnout: An Investigation of a Model. *Dissertation Abstracts International*, Vol. 47, No. 4, P. 1768B.

House, J.S., (1974); Occupational Stress and Coronary Heart Disease: A Review and Theoretical Integration. *Journal of Health and Social Behaviour*, 15, 12-27.

House, R.H., & Rizzo, J.R (1972); Role Conflict and Ambiguity as Critical Variables in a Model of Organisational Behaviour. *Organisational Behaviour and Human Performance*, 7, 467-505.

Howard, J.H., Cunningham, D.A., Rechnilzer, P.A., & Goode, R.C (1976); Stress in the Job and Career of a Dentist. *Journal of the American Dental Association*, 93, 630-636.

Indik, B., Seachore, S. E & Slesinger, J (1964); Demographic Correlates of Psychological Strain. *Journal of Abnormal and Social Psychology*, 69, 26-38.

Jackson, S.E., (1983); Participation in Decision-making as a Strategy for Reducing Job-related Strain. *Journal of Applied Psychology*, 68, 3-19.

Jains, I.L., & Katz, D (1959): The Reduction of Intergroup Hostility, Research Problems and Hypotheses. *Journal of Conflict Resolution*, 3, 85-100.

Jamal, M., (1984); Job Stress and Job Performance Controversy: An Empirical Assessment. *Organisational Behaviour and Human Performance*, 33, 1-21.

Jayabal G, (2004); Strategic Management of Stress for Better Performance, *Personnel Today*, January-March, 2004, pp. 40-43.

Jayakumar, P, Muralidharan, K, Ashok Kumar, M, (2006); Job Satisfaction and Job Stress Among I.T. Employees, *Organisational Management*, Vol. XXII, No. 3, Oct-Dec. 2006, pp. 12-15.

Johnson, T.W., & Stinson, J.E., (1975); Role Ambiguity, *Role Conflict and Satisfaction: Moderating Effects of Individual Differences Journal of Applied Psychology*, 60, 329-333.

Kahn, R.L., (1978); Job Burnout: Prevention and Remedies. *Public Welfare*, 16, 61-63.

Keenan, A., & Mcbain, G.D.M (1979); Effects of Type A Behaviour, Intolerance of Ambiguity and Locus of Control on the Relationship Between Role Stress and Work-related Outcomes. *Journal of Occupational Psychology*, 52, 277-285.

Kohn, M.L., (1976): Occupational Sources and Alienation. *American Journal of Sociology*. Vol. 82, No. 1, 111-130.

Krishnamoorthy, K.N., (2003): Stress on 'Co-operative' Traffic Management, *Motor India*, Vol. 47, No. 8, March, 2003, p. 47.

Lakhwinder Singh Kang, Raghbir Singh, (2004); Identifying Stressors at Work—A Case of Employees in the Electronics Industry, *Decision*, Vol. 31, No. 1, January-June, 2004, pp. 51-72.

Litterer, J.A., (1966); Conflict in Organisations: A Re-examination. *Academy of Management Journal*, 9, 178-186.

Manimaran S, Hari Sundar G, (2006), Job Stress in Business Organisations: Causes, Consequences and Coping Strategies, *Organisational Management*, Vol. XXIII, No. 3, Oct-Dec. 2006, pp. 38-42

Margolis, G.L., Kroes, W.H., & Quinn, R.P (1974); Job Stress: An Unlisted Occupational Hazard. *Journal of Occupational Medicine*, 16, 659-661.

Maslach, C & Jackson. S.E., (1982); Burnout in the Health Professions: A Social Psychological Analysis. In G. Sandess & S.Suls (Ed.). *Social Psychology of Health and Illness*, Hillsdale, NJ: Erlbaum

Maslach, C & Jackson. S.E., (1984); Patterns of Burnout Among a National Sample of Public Contact Workers. *Journal of Health and Human Resources Administration*.

Maslach, C & Jackson. S.E., (1985); The Role of Sex and Family Variables in Burnout. *Sex Roles*, 12, 837-851.

Maslach, C & Pines, A., (1977); The Burn-out Syndrome in the Day Care Setting. *Child Care Quarterly*, 6, 100-113.

Matteson, M.T., & Ivancevich, J.M (1979); Organisational Stressors and Heart Disease: A Research Model. *Academy of Management Review*, 4, 347-357.

Mazur, P., (1987); Burnout: The Relationship Between the Principal's Leadership Style, the Organisation, and the Teacher's Personality. *Dissertation Abstracts International* Vol. 47, No. 8, P. 2831A.

McCarthy, H., & Schaar, J.H (1965); Psychological Dimensions of Anomie, *American Sociological Review*, 30, 14-40.

Merton, R.K (1940); Bureaucratic Structure and Personality. *Social Forces*, 17, 560-569.

Michailidis Maria, Georgiou Yiota, (2005); Employee Occupational Stress in Banking, *Work* 24 (2005) pp. 123-137.

Miles, R.H., (1975); An Empirical Test of Casual Inference Between Role Perception of Conflict and Ambiguity and Various Personal Outcomes. *Journal of Applied Psychology*, 60, 334-339.

Milgram, S., (1965); Some Conditions of Obedience and Disobedience to Authority. *Human Relations*, 18, 57-76.

Morris, J.H. and Koch, J.L (1979); Impact of Role Perceptions on Organisational Commitment, Job Involvement and Psychosomatic Illness Among Three Vocational Groupings. *Journal of Vocational Behaviour*, 14, 88-101.

Morries, J.H., & Snyder, R.A (1979); A Second Look at Need for Achievement and Need for Autonomy As Moderators of Role Perception—Outcome Relationships. *Journal of Applied Psychology*, 64, 173-178.

Morries, J.H., Streers R.M., & Koch J.L., (1979); Influence of Organisation Structure on Role Conflict and Ambiguity for Three Occupational Groupings. *Academy of Management Journal*, 22, 58-71.

Narayanan, S., (1983b); Contribution of Religion to Probabilistic Orientation. *Paper Presented to the National Seminar on Current Issues of Philosophy of Religion*, Christian College, Madras.

Narayanan, S., (1983c); Role Conflict Differential (RCD): A Direct Method of Assessing the Role Conflict. *Unpublished Research Paper*, Bharathiar University, Coimbatore.

Narayanan, S., (1984); Probabilistic Orientation and Level of Aspiration. *Unpublished Research Paper,* Bharathiar University, Coimbatore.

Narayanan, S., (1985a); Probabilistic Orientation and Mental Health, *Unpublished Research Paper,* Bharathiar University.

Narayanan, S., (1985b); Probabilistic Orientation and MMPI. *Paper Presented at the Indian Psychilatric Conference.*

Narayanan, S., (1986); Probabilistic Orientation in Relation to Personal Values. *Unpublished Research Paper*, Bharathiar University.

Narayanan, S., Venkatapathy, R & Govindarasu.S., (1984); Locus of Control and Probabilistic Orientation, *Psychological Studies*, 29, 1, 68-70.

Narayanan, S., & Govindarasu, S., (1986a); Probabilistic Orientation and Security-Insecurity, *Psychological Research Journal*, Vol. 10, Nos. 1&2., 1-7.

Neal, A.G., & Retting, S., (1963); On the Multi-Dimensionality of Alienation. *American Sociological Review*, 32, 54-64.

Neal, A.G., & Retting, S., (1967); Organisations and Powerlessness: A Test of the Mediation Hypothesis. *American Sociological Review*, 29, 216-226.

Nettler, G., (1957); A Measure of Alienation. *American Sociological Review*, 22, 670-677.

Organ, D.W., & Greene, C.N., (1974); Role Ambiguity, Locus of Control and Work Satisfaction. *Journal of Applied Psychology*, 59, 101-102.

Parsons, T., (1968); "Pareto, Vilfredo": Contributions to *Sociology, International Encyclopedia of the Social Sciences*, II, 414-415.

Pearline, L.I (1962); Alienation from Work: A Study of Nursing Personnel, *American Sociological Review*, 27, 314-326.

Pestonjee, D.M., & Singh, A.K., (1978); Alienation and Dogmatism in Indian Youth: A Correlational Study. *Psychological Studies*, 23, 87-90.

Pines, A., & Maslach, C (1978); Characteristics of Staff Burnout in Mental Health Settings. *Hospital and Community Psychiatry*, 29, 233-237.

Porter, L.W., & Steers, R.M. (1973); Organisational, Work and Personal Factors in Employee Turnover and Absenteeism. *Psychological Bulletin*, 80, 151-176.

Porter, L.W., & Steers, R.M., Mowday, R.T. , & Boulian, P.V., (1974); Organisational Commitment, Job Satisfaction and Turnover Among Psychiatric Technicians. *Journals of Applied Psychology*, 19, 475-479.

Rajeswari K.S., Anantharaman, R.N.,(2003); Role of Need for Clarity in the Relationship Between Occupational Stress and Work Exhaustion Among Software Professionals, *Management and Change*, Vol. 7, No. 2, 2003, pp. 207-225.

Ramey, J.W., (1972); Commune, Group Marriages and the Upper Middle-Class. *Journal of Marriage and the Family*, 34, 647-655.

Rapoport, A., (1966); Models of Conflict: Cataclysmic and Strategic. In A. De Reuck & J. Knight (Eds.), *Conflict in Society*. Boston: Little, Brown, 259-288.

Reetz, L.J., (1985); Burnout Among Rural Special Education Specialists: An Investigation of Selected Variables. *Dissertation Abstracts International*, Vol. 45, No. 8, P. 2488A.

Rizzo, J.R., House R.J Lirtzman, S., (1970); Role Conflict and Ambiguity in Organisation. *Administrative Science Quarterly*, 15, 15-163.

Rotter, J.B., (1966); Generalised Expectancies for Internal Versus External Control of Reinforcement. *Psychological Monographs*, 80-1, (Whole) No. 609.

Ruzzek, H.I., & Russek, L.G., (1976); Is Emotional Stress an Etiological Factor in Coronary Heart Disease? *Psychometrics* 17,63-67.

Russell. D. W., Altmaier, E., & Volzen. D.V., (1987); Job Related Stress Social Support and Burnout Among Class Room Teacher. *Journal of Applied Psychology*, 72, 2, 269-274.

Sales, S.M (1969); Organisational Role as a Risk Factor in Coronary Disease. *Administrative Science Quarterly*, 14, 325-336.

Scherer, S.E., Ettinger, R.E., & Murdick, N.J., (1972); Need for Social Approved and Drug Use. *Journal of Consulting and Clinical Psychology*, 38, 118-121.

Schill, J., (1972); Need for Approval, Guilt and Sexual Stimulation and Their Relationship to Sexual Responsibility, *Journal of Consulting and Clinical Psychology*, 38, 31-35.

Schuler, R.S. (1975); Role Perceptions, Satisfaction and Performance: A Partial Reconciliation. *Journal of Applied Psychology*, 60, 683-687.

Shinn, M., Rosario, M., Morch, H., & Chestnut, D.E, (1984); Coping with Job Stress and Burnout in the Human Services. *Journal of Personality and Social Psychology*, 46, 864-876.

Siegel, S.M and Kolmmerr, H., (1976); Measuring the Perceived Support for Innovation in Organisations. *Journal of Applied Psychology*, Vol. 63, No. 5, pp. 553-562.

Singh, B., Agarwala, U.N. & Malhan, N.K (1981); The Nature of Managerial Role Conflict. *Indian Journal of Industrial Relations* 17,1, 1-26.

Singhal C.S., Yogananda Sastry, Vijayakumar S, (2002); Course on Strategies for Management of Stress in Organisations, Centre for Behavioural and Organisational Development, National Institute of Rural Development, Rajendranagar, Hyderabad.

Snoek, J.D (1966); Role Strain in Diversified Role Sets. *American Journal of Sociology*, 71, 363-372.

Srinivasan P.T., David Jawahar P., (2003); Empowerment as a Moderator of the Relationship Between Work Stress and Psychosomatic Symptoms, *The Icfaian Journal of Organisational Behaviour*, Oct. 2003.

Swaminathan M, (2003); Stress Management, *Tamil Nadu Journal of Co-operation*, Feb. 2003, pp. 11-15.

Thaw, J., & Efren J.S., (1967); The Relationship of Need for Approval to Decensiveness and Goal Setting Behaviour: A Partial Replication. *Journal of Psychology*, 65, 41.

Tosi, H & Tosi D., (1970); Some Correlates of Role and Ambiguity Among Public School Teachers. *Journal of Human Relations*, 18, 1063-1975.

Ursprung, A.W., (1984); Dimensions of Burnout in Residential Service Workers. *Dissertation Abstracts International*, Vol. 45, No. 2, p. 473A.

Walpole, B.R., (1984); Burnout Reduction Among Registered Nurses Through an Educational Treatment Programme. *Dissertation Abstracts International*, Vol.45, No. 4, P. 1013A.

Whitehead, J.T (1987); Probation Officer Job Burnout: A Test of Two Theories. *Journal of Criminal Justice*. Vol. 15, 1-16.

Wolfe, D.M., & Snock, J.D (1962); A Study of Tensions and Adjustments Under Role Conflict. *Journal of Social Issues*, 18, 102-121.

## UNPUBLISHED THESIS

Augustine, V.D (1978); Mental Health of Industrial Worker. *Unpublished Master of Philosophy Dissertation*, University of Madras.

Balakrishanan, R., (1985); A Study of Motivational and Personality Characteristics of Entrepreneurs. *Unpublished Doctor of Philosophy Dissertation*, Bharathiar University.

Beena, C.J., (1987); A Study on Work, Family, Inter Role Conflict and Their Relation to Personality and Life-Related Outcomes. *Unpublished Master of Arts Dissertation*, PSG College of Arts and Science, Coimbatore.

Burke, J.M., (1985); The Relationship Between Type a Behaviour, Role Stress, Job Enrichment and Burnout Among College Counsellors. *Unpublished Doctor of Philosophy Dissertation*, Texas A & M University.

Davis—Sacks, M.<., (1985); the Effects of Job-Specific Role Stresses and Personal Control on Burnout and Other Psychological Strains Among Child Welfare Workers. *Unpublished Doctor of Philosophy Dissertation*, University of Michigan.

Devi, S.R., (1982); A Study of Role Conflict in Relation to Anxiety Clienation and Probabilistic Orientation. *Unpublished Master of Philosophy Dissertation*, University of Madras.

Gann, M.L., (1979); The Role of Personality Factors and Job Characteristics in Burnout: A Study of Social Service Workers. *Unpublished Doctoral Dissertation*, University of California, Berkeley.

Govindarasu, S., (1984); A Study of Accidents Among Transport Drivers in Relation to Certain Cognitive Styles. *Unpublished Master of Philosophy Dissertation*, Bharathiar University.

Holt, P., (1985); A Study of the Interaction of Levels of Occupational Stress, Degree of Burnout and Personality Hardiness in Female Elementary Teachers. *Unpublished Doctor of Philosophy Dissertation*, University of Kansas.

Hubert, J.A., (1984); The Relationship of School Organisational Health and Teacher Need Satisfaction to Teacher Stress. *Unpublished Doctor of Philosophy Dissertation*, University of Connecticut.

Indumathi, K., (1988); Job Reactions Under Different Systems of Management Among Textile Organisations. *Unpublished Doctor of Philosophy Thesis*. Bharathiar University.

Jayaraj, M., (1984); A Study of Probabilistic Orientation in Relation to Innovative Personality, Perceived Support for Innovation, Mental Health and Sex. *Unpublished Master of Philosophy Dissertation*. Bharathiar University.

Narayanan, S., (1975); A Study of Fatigue and Related Extraversion Introversion and Neuroticism in an Industrial Setting. *Unpublished Doctor of Philosophy Dissertation*, University of Madras.

Rajasekharan, D., (1980); Personality and Role Strain, *Unpublished Master of Arts Dissertation*, PSG College of Arts & Science, Coimbatore.

Schweb, R.L., (1981); The Relationship of Role Conflict, Role Ambiguity Teacher Background Variables and Perceived Burnout Among Teachers. (*Doctoral Dissertation, University of Connecticut*) DAI, 41(09-A)2, 3823-a.

Saranya, A.S., (1999), Job Stress of Bank Employees, *Unpublished Doctoral Thesis*, University of Madras, Chennai.

Sunandini, P., (1985); A Study of the Personality of Housewives Career Women and Women Entrepreneurs. *Unpublished Doctor of Philosophy Dissertation*, Bharathiar University.

Synthia (1988); Personality Types and Probabilistic Orientation, *Unpublished Master of Philosophy Dissertation*, Bharathiar University.

Venkatachalam, R., (1978); A Study of Innovation in Relation to Personlity, Situational Constraints and Reinforcements Involved in Industrial Setting. *Unpublished Master of Phiosophy Dissertation*, University of Madras.

**REPORTS**

Barad, C.B., (1979); Study of Burnout Syndrome Among Social Security Administration Field Public Contact Employees. *Unpublished Report, Social Security Administration.*

Census of India (1981); Series – 20. Tamil Nadu, Part II, *Special Report and Table Based on 5 Per Cent Sample Data*. Office of the Registrar General & Census Commissioner, India.

Etzion, D., & Pines. A., (1981); Burnout and Coping: A Cross-Cultural Cross-Sexual Comparison. *Paper Presented at the International Interdisciplinary Conference on Women*, Haifa, Israel.

Friedman, M., (1978); Type a Behaviour, and Your Heart. *Paper Presented at Conference on the Nature and Management of Stress*. Santacruz: University of Califormia Extension, April.

*IV Pay Commission Report*, (1984); Government Press, Government of Tamil Nadu.

Jackson, S.E., & Maslach, C., (1980); Job Stress Among Helping Professionals: The Effects on Workers and Their Families. *Paper Presented at the Research Workshop on Current Issues in Occupational Stress: Theory, Research and Intervention*, Downs View, Ontario.

**WEBSITES**

www.spinelife.com

www.extension.umn.edu

www.livetinc.com

www.touchlocal.com

www.reliefweb.int

www.funcilitators.com

www.falconbury.co.uk

www.indiaeducation.info

www.managementhelp.org

www.nexport.com

www.blogsource.org

www.stress-vacation.com

# Index

**T**



**W**



❑❑❑